NEWNESS
OF LIFE

NEWNESS OF LIFE

New Light from the Gospel of John

Estelle C. Carver

Edited by
Hal M. Helms

Paraclete Press
Orleans, Massachusetts

This book was originally published by the Division of Women's Service of the Board of Missions of the United Methodist Church, and is republished with their permission, with minor editorial changes.

To my father and mother,
who early set my feet in
the path of prayer and praise.

About the Author

Estelle Carver was born of English parents in Jamaica, British West Indies on Holy Innocents' Day, December 28, 1890. Her name, "Estelle," was given because the Christmas star was still shining on her birthday. Her Hertfordshire great-grandfather and grandfather had gone out as missionaries to Antigua and Jamaica.

Drawn to Christ by her parents, she early showed a keen interest in the Bible and a love for the Book of Common Prayer of the Church of England. Before coming to the United States, Miss Carver had taught English and religious knowledge in Jamaican high schools. In 1923 she began to teach in New Haven, Connecticut, and in 1931 became an instructor in English at Hopkins Grammar School, a college preparatory school for boys, founded in 1660 by Edward Hopkins, governor of Connecticut. She filled this position with distinction for twenty-four years, and is described by colleagues as "a powerful teacher who got everything out of the students they had to give."

She did graduate work at Columbia University and at Bread Loaf School of English at Middlebury College, Vermont. For two years she lectured in the Department of Education at Yale University.

Her chief interest besides English was Religious Education, especially in the field of prayer and the development of the spiritual life. In 1941 she worked with the Very Reverend Dr. William Palmer Ladd, dean of Berkeley Divinity School in New Haven, in organizing the "Prayer Guild for War Time." In the course of time she was invited to conduct schools of prayer, Lenten courses, quiet days and retreats, and to assist at youth conferences.

On her retirement from Hopkins in 1955, Miss Carver devoted full time to her efforts to promote a deeper spiritual life in the churches. At the invitation of Bishop William Appleton Lawrence, she became Resource Person for Retreats, Quiet Days and Bible Study for the Episcopal Diocese of Western Massachusetts, and in that capacity served for many years at Lasell House in Whitinsville, Massachusetts.

A friend in Greenwich, Connecticut made a practice of inviting Miss Carver to teach a small group of guests in her home every year. Rev. and Mrs. H. Arthur Lane and others from St. Paul's Church, Darien, heard her at Mrs. Kramer's in 1967, and proceeded to invite her to teach each year at St. Paul's. It was through the Lanes that Miss Carver paid her first visit to the Community of Jesus, and it was "love at first sight" on both sides. She found that her own spirituality corresponded closely to that of the founders of the Community, M. Cay Andersen and M. Judy Sorensen, and that, like Jonathan and David, "their souls were knit as one." From then on, she came at least twice a year to teach various sections of the Bible and to lecture on the riches of the Book of Common Prayer, and at other times simply for rest and personal renewal.

In 1975 she became the first Honorary Member of the Community, and spent her last birthday there, saying it was the place she loved best in the world. Returning home to the Retirement Center in Alexandria, Virginia, (where she had been instrumental in starting a Bible study among the residents), she did not respond to calls from a friend who planned to take her to lunch on January 8, 1976. Going to Miss Carver's apartment, the friend found her lifeless body, sitting with her Bible open to Psalm 119, which she was in the process of memorizing at the age of 86.

A favorite story she sometimes told concerned the death of John Wesley, whom she greatly admired. Wesley had lived to the ripe old age of 88, and lying on his death-bed, he raised his head, with the words, "I'll praise...." But his strength failed, and his head sank. A little while later, he revived, and held his head up again, saying, "I'll praise...." But strength failed again. A third time, he spoke the words, "I'll praise..." and was gone.

Miss Carver said, "What John Wesley was trying to quote was a line from a favorite hymn of his, Isaac Watts' "I'll praise my Maker while I've breath..." Then she would go on to quote the first stanza, as follows:

> I'll praise my Maker while I've breath
> And when my voice is lost in death
> Praise shall employ my nobler powers.
> My days of praise shall ne'er be past
> While life, and thought or being last
> Or immortality endures.

Then she added, "What a wonderful way to die—with a triple Praise on his lips!"

Miss Carver believed strongly in the value of memorization—of Scripture, hymns, and good poetry. One of her favorite words of counsel: "Never waste precious time by reading a trashy book. Fill the storehouse of your thoughts with treasures." And she lived what she taught.

It is a great joy to offer to the Christian public this little book, filled with sound learning and the warm devotion and distilled wisdom of a wholly committed life, whose one aim was to lift up and glorify Jesus Christ. She, "being dead, yet speaketh." (Hebrews 11:4)

Hal M. Helms

Author's Introduction

The time is ripe for a revival of Christian faith and practice throughout the world. In England and in America spiritual leaders are engaged in a great evangelical movement—a vigorous attempt to recapture the vitality of the gospel message—the only hope of our world.

It is evident that God has laid His hand on the leaders of various branches of His "Holy Church throughout the world," bidding them in words of burning conviction, "Speak to the Church, that she go forward!"

But new names on the membership roll of any church can mean little if members are merely nominal Christians. Church membership, to be vital and nation-shaking, must mean, in the stalwart phraseology of the early Church, conviction, repentance, conversion, regeneration, consecration— a walking in that "newness of life" which was the goal of first-century evangelism that "turned the world upside down."

The aim of this booklet is to serve as a guide for Church members, new and old, showing how true Christian living, which is "newness of life," may be developed in the lives of all who come to Jesus with an earnest desire to be built up as living cells in His Body, the Church. It suggests a way in which our hearts may be prepared for that gift of new life which the Holy Spirit offers bountifully to all who are receptive to His invasion. This practical way of growth is based on the seven "Signs" recorded in the first twelve chapters of St. John's Gospel.

St. John uses a Greek word which means "sign" for the miracles of our Lord, instead of the Greek word for "wonder," which the writers of the other Gospels use.[1] He saw each miracle, not as a display of wonder and power, but as a sign— an outward act that points to an inner meaning—an activity of Jesus which shows forth the glory of God and His great love for us.

From early childhood I have been interested in these Signs. My father's frequent discussion of Bishop Westcott's commentary, *The Gospel According to St. John,* on the symbolism of these Signs as a means of personal spiritual growth, kindled my imagination and led me to read them again and again, and, as I grew older, to study them with the aid of many commentaries and expositions written by great spiritual scholars, from whom I have received illumination and rich interpretations.

The development of the spiritual life has a twofold aspect: love of God and service to man. Our Lord's glad spending of Himself, demonstrated throughout the Gospels, must characterize our discipleship also. We pledge ourselves to "an unconditional and filial devotion to the interests of God."[1] Such devotion will compel us to relate our spiritual life to the needs of the world. Let us, therefore, pause before we begin the study of each chapter and pray the Holy Spirit to brood upon our hearts so that we may grow in grace and bring forth the fruit of sacrificial service, which is the only sure sign of newness of life.

Prayer suggested for use before each chapter:

Heavenly Father, we pray Thee to illumine our minds and hearts with the bright light of Thy Holy Spirit, that we may grasp the teachings which Thy beloved disciple and evangelist, St. John, sets forth in this Sign of _____. *(Here name the Sign.)* Help us to show forth in our daily lives the light of Thy truth which Thou dost reveal; through Jesus Christ our Lord. Amen.

---

[1] The American Revised Version and other translations make this distinction clearer than does the King James Version.

Unless otherwise indicated, the biblical quotations in this book have been taken from the King James Version.

[1] Evelyn Underhill, *Abba* (London: Longmans, Green and Co., Ltd., 1940), p. 10.

CONTENTS

Chapter One

New Birth

John 2:1-11

(The Marriage at Cana)

And the third day there was a marriage in Cana of Galilee; and the mother of Jesus was there: and both Jesus was called, and His disciples, to the marriage. And when they wanted wine, the mother of Jesus saith unto Him, They have no wine. Jesus saith unto her, Woman, what have I to do with thee? Mine hour is not yet come. His mother saith unto the servants, Whatsoever He saith unto you, do it. And there were set there six waterpots of stone, after the manner of the purifying of the Jews, containing two or three firkins apiece. Jesus saith unto them, Fill the waterpots with water. And they filled them up to the brim. And He saith unto them, Draw out now, and bear unto the governor of the feast. And they bare it. When the ruler of the feast had tasted the water that was made wine, and knew not whence it was: (but the servants which drew the water knew;) the governor of the feast called the bridegroom, and saith unto him, Every man at the beginning doth set forth good wine; and when men have well drunk, then that which is worse: but thou hast kept the good wine until now. This beginning of miracles did Jesus in Cana of Galilee, and manifested forth His glory; and His disciples believed on Him.

$\mathcal{I}$n the beginning God . . . ." Thus does the inspired Hebrew writer state the origin of our physical universe; the spiritual growth of each individual starts in the same way. The Hebrews did see the Creator and Sustainer of all life as the Father of Israel, and in this limited fatherhood, prophets and psalmists, in the highest and tenderest reaches of their faith, did glimpse, in embryo, "Father of all mankind." But only the Son could reveal the full glad act of God as Father and proclaim His world-embracing love! Thus Jesus, in His infinite tenderness, illuminates the awe-inspiring word "God." He lifts the veil from it, and while in no wise diminishing the sense of reverential awe that God demands, He reveals the Reality for whom the word stands — a Name, a Being having characteristics of personality, and the properties of warmth, closeness, and tenderness, so that we can come to God and say with childlike trust, "In the beginning, Father!" It was the wonder of this fulness of "Father!" that brought forth Charles Wesley's rapturous cry:

> 'Tis Love! 'tis Love! Thou diedst for me!
>   I hear Thy whisper in my heart;
> The morning breaks, the shadows flee;
>   Pure, universal love Thou art:
> To me, to all, Thy mercies move;
>   Thy nature and Thy Name is Love.

The gospel is good tidings from and concerning our Heavenly Father. The very name "father" united us into a family, and we see Jesus at the beginning of His ministry moving in a natural and intimate way amid home surroundings. He shows forth His Father's glory in a home, the place where life normally begins, laying the foundation of holy living amid laughter and fellowship and wedding festivities, as two young would-be homemakers are being joyously "joined together in holy matrimony" for the Godlike responsibilities of family life. What a glorious setting for the gospel message!

15

With inspired insight the author of the Fourth Gospel grasped the significance of this basic Sign of enrichment. Baron Von Hugel, in his instructions for a life of prayer, puts this fact first. *"God is a stupendously rich Reality . . . .* Our prayer will lack the deepest awe and widest expansion if we do not find room within it for this fact concerning God."[1]

Jesus in Our Homes

Jesus comes into our homes in response, perhaps, to a very casual invitation, but before we are fully aware of the Presence of the Wonderful One in our midst, everything in our homes becomes enriched through transformation. The daily routine, with its joys, sorrows, anxieties, undergoes a heart-change. Life ceases to be insipid and silly, for "Nothing has taste unless Jesus is in it." Words that we have heard over and over again begin "to quicken and to shine" with new meaning. "I am come that they might have life, and that they might have it more abundantly."[2] Look up the derivation of the word "abundantly" — the vivid keynote of this first Sign. It is in itself a picture of what the spiritual life is — wave upon wave rolling in to us from the great ocean of God's Spirit, a never-failing, rhythmic giving of Himself, and, as though that regular, deliberate, sufficient inflow were not enough, there is the great ocean swell of the "ninth wave," symbolic of that "full measure, running over" which is the outstanding characteristic of our Heavenly Father's love.

As Host and Permanent Guest

The Savior can no longer be looked upon or treated as a casual or transient guest. We long to have Him as a permanent member of the family. St. Augustine gives us the perfect

[1] Baron Friedrich Von Hugel. *The Life of Prayer* (New York: E. P. Dutton & Co., Inc., 1929), p. 8.
[2] John 10:10

pattern of invitation: "Thou art come, Lord Jesus, into the house of my soul. I will not play the host to Thee as to a stranger. Rather art *Thou* the Host and Master, and I Thy guest, since Thou dost provide the banquet, and the house belongs to Thee." So we build a little room for Him as the Shunammite woman did for Elisha — a little room, emptied and swept, not cluttered up with our belongings that leave no room for the Guest, but furnished with the bare necessities that are symbolic of the simplicity that He brings to our complicated lives: a bed, that He may stay with us when the day is far spent, and the night watches begin; a table, that He may be our Guest at every meal, and be ever more intimately known to us in the breaking of bread; a stool, that we may sit often at His feet and learn of Him and have "sweet discourse..., ...pleasant solace, much peace and an intimate closeness, exceeding wonderful"[1]; and finally a candlestick, that He may be our Light and our Guide, dispelling darkness, revealing dangers, and solving perplexities — transforming our everyday living into a more golden way.

As Master and Lord

Invitation, enrichment, abiding! Have we been sincere in telling Him that the house belongs to Him? If we have really meant it, then He will take us at our word and take control as Master and Lord. His Presence in our hearts and homes will stab us broad awake and make us acutely conscious of our greatest need — a need that we have not liked to think about too seriously — but on the recognition of which the whole glad transformation of our life depends, a need that is implicit in His dearest name of all — "And thou shalt call His name JESUS: for He shall save His people from their sins."[2] The

---

[1]Thomas a Kempis, *The Imitation of Christ.* Ed. by Hal M. Helms; Revised translation (Paraclete Press, 1982), Book II, p. 81.
[2]Matt. 1:21

word "sin" has almost become obsolete in our humanitarian approach to religion. But we have no knowledge and no need of JESUS until sin becomes the stark fact of our lives and of our world. The spiritual masters of our faith have steadfastly held, as did Mary of Bethany, to that "one thing needful" — a recognition of the satanic power of sin, a force so sinister that it made the Triumphal Entry of our Lord a procession, not from Bethany to Jerusalem — as the happy crowds with their superficial thinking blindly imagined — but from Jerusalem to Calvary, His sweet name of Savior compelling Him along that way to death and burial.

As Cleanser of Our Hearts

Sir Edwyn Hoskyns states in his scholarly book, *The Fourth Gospel,* that the very fact that water-pots were in the home at Cana for purification was a reminder that all was not well there.[1] The first essential need of every heart and home is cleansing. We can bravely affirm that science and hygiene and a certain type of shallow, popular psychology have now antiquated the line in one of our truest and most poignant hymns: "Frail children of dust, and feeble as frail";[2] but when we are honest with ourselves, we know that the strong, vigorous Anglo-Saxon verb which begins the petition in the exquisite "Collect for Purity" is the cry that comes to our lips when we are face to face with Jesus. "Cleanse!" You may remember in *Brother Saul* by Donn Byrne how Saul's somewhat reprobate and crafty, yet wise, influential, and lovable "Uncle Joachim," fascinated and disturbed by the things he had heard about the young lad Jesus, went to see him, all prepared to test Jesus with "questions of practice and polity, men's questions." He found Jesus planing a plank of wood in his father's workshop:

---

[1] Cf. Edwyn Hoskyns, *The Fourth Gospel* (Ed. by Francis Noel Davey; Second Edition revised; London: Faber & Faber, Ltd., 1947), p. 186.
[2] Robert Grant, "O Worship the King, All Glorious Above."

"He had a face sweet as a girl's, but a man's face, and eyes so clear that I felt dirty. 'Are you Jesus?' I asked. 'What do you wish of me?' he said." — Then old Joachim, who had talked to Tiberius, as man to man and had made known to the Emperor "the real truth about things in Asia," says simply: "But when I saw that young man — just a boy, Saul, not two years older than you! — I said, 'I'd like a drink of water.' . . . He's good, my dear; you can feel it in the air where he is."[1]

Yes, when we look into those eyes, we, too, feel dirty, and we cry, "Cleanse!" A truly devout Christian woman, who spends her life loving God and serving His children, once came up to me after she had heard me speak on that collect, which is at the beginning of the service of Holy Communion, and said humbly: "That's the only word. I keep on saying it over and over. 'Cleanse! Cleanse! Cleanse!'" She was sharing the experience that comes to everyone who, like Isaiah, has seen "the Lord high and lifted up" and knows the reality of the "smoke" — the cloud barrier created by the impurity in our lives. The first cry of the young Isaiah, doubtless in his day the finest and most clear-sighted of the citizens in Jerusalem, was, "Woe to me!" when he knew God as an actuality. "Unclean" — that repulsive word, associated as it was throughout Hebrew history with the loathsome disease of leprosy — was the only adequate adjective the young prophet could find to express his sinfulness and that of his nation, in that moment of wondrous vision of the holiness of God.

"Cleanse the thoughts of our hearts by the inspiration of Thy Holy Spirit!"[2] When that cry comes simply yet agonizingly to our lips, we know that we have found Jesus. The very fact that the three great cleansing agents of our physical universe — Water, Fire, Wind — are used as symbols of the Holy Spirit shows that cleansing is His first great business

---

[1]Donn Byrne, *Brother Saul* (New York: The Century Co., 1927), p. 65.
[2]Collect for Purity from *The Book of Common Prayer*.

in our lives. "Lo, this hath touched thy lips; and thy iniquity is taken away, and thy sin is purged."[1] "I will; be thou clean."[2] We have only to ask for cleansing, and it comes, swiftly and completely. Then He takes control of the cleansed heart and the cleansed home, and the experience of His cleansing power will be to us a miracle of love at which we shall never cease to marvel.

As Guide and Pattern

Enrichment, cleansing — these first steps are followed by the continued action of the Holy Spirit in reordering our lives according to His will. Our home is now His. Family prayers are now the "house-band" — that wise word of unifying strength which suggests what a husband is intended to be in a home — father, mother, children, guests, helpers, all banded into one and held together by the strong bands of prayer. Grace at meals becomes a regular habit, creating a mood of loving gratitude toward our Heavenly Father. Food simply cannot be eaten without a blessing, at a table at which Jesus is Guest! To thank God for His bounty leads us on to a thoughtful recognition of those who prepare our food or who serve us in any other capacity in our homes; then reaching out beyond ourselves, we strive to fulfil our obligations to Him by passing on His bounty in whatever way we can to His needy children in neighborhood, nation, or world. Meals eaten in such an atmosphere of gratitude, thoughtfulness, and love are indeed thrice-blessed.

Thus home — in the family and in the individual heart — becomes "a nourishing and cherishing mother" — an environment in which love is actively present. The mother of Jesus had so ordered her home that her Child could grow in that four-square perfection — physical, intellectual, spiritual, social — which is the dearest hope of every father and mother

[1] Isa. 6:7
[2] Luke 5:13

who is not content to be merely a parent. My father used to say that fathers and mothers are those who have children — sons and daughters — and that parents are those who have offspring. Institutions for the prevention of cruelty to children are made necessary by the second group — never by the first. In Christian homes the names "father" and "mother" have their deepest meaning and most solemn obligations. "And Jesus increased in wisdom and stature, and in favour with God and man."[1] His mother had trained and guided Him in the performance of those duties that fall to every child in a well-ordered home. In the account of this Sign we discover the secret of successful homemaking in her injunction to the servants — obedience to the will of God. "Whatsoever He saith unto you, do it."[2] These words should be written deeply in the heart of every member of a family. His mother had known Him intimately for thirty years, and her confidence in Him had never been shaken. What she had not understood, she pondered the wonder of His birth and of Him, and had still trusted. There could be no greater tribute paid to any son than the implicit faith in Him that her words express. "Whatsoever" is not a word to be uttered lightly. If every married couple through daily prayer together would make that injunction the cornerstone of their married life — repeating it as a renewal of their vows — "Whatsoever He saith unto us, through His Grace, we will do" — divorce would cease to be a tragic commonplace in our nation. A home in which God is Father and Guide, in which father and mother seek to be patterned after the Heavenly Father whom Jesus revealed, and in which trustful and complete obedience to the will of Jesus is the ruling characteristic, can never become a broken home. Death does not break a home. Shutting God out of a home breaks it.

[1]Luke 2:52
[2]John 2:5

Results of Enrichment

Enrichment — such as "eye hath not seen nor ear heard" — is thus the first phase of a life of spiritual growth, and this "Abundant Living" (to quote the title of one of Dr. E. Stanley Jones's most helpful little books) is brought about by the Presence and action of Jesus in our hearts — through cleansing, reordering, and prayer — and is made perfect through obedience. His will, not ours, is the first decisive choice. If we begin by receiving and obeying Jesus, selfishness in personal devotion becomes an impossibility, for a robust spiritual life develops in association with others, as we grow and love and share in the life of a family. God in His gracious planning has emphasized the necessity of a home, for He "setteth the solitary in families,"[1] giving to the unmarried, homes in which they can truly belong. What a glad way of growth is this! an all-round development brought about by the "give and take" in family relationships.

In an old scrapbook of my father's, I chanced as a child upon some words destined to stay with me. The author is forgotten, but I remember the words. Even to my child-mind they aroused a feeling of joy, and I kept reading them again and again. As I grew up with them, they seemed to create a setting of gladness and expectancy that linked the home in Eden with the home in Cana, and then swept on to Patmos with its vision of the home and marriage supper of the Lamb: "The Gospel is an anthem from the gates of heaven, the music of the River of Life pouring in cascades of harmony upon the earth; first uttered in Eden by the Lord Himself — when He gave the keynote of the Gospel song: the coming of His anointed for the redemption of His people and for the glory of His holy name!" What a joyous, bell-like symphony of newness of life, beginning and ending in natural family celebrations — a wedding feast and a marriage supper!

Let us read and ponder this great first Sign in Cana of

[1]Psalm 68:6.

Galilee. Then let us lift up our hearts to Jesus and say quite simply,

> O come to my heart, Lord Jesus.
> There is room in my heart for Thee.

And before the invitation has found utterance, He will have entered and taken up His abode with us.

Chapter Two

Learning to Trust

John 4:46-54

(The Healing of the Nobleman's Son)

So Jesus came again into Cana of Galilee, where He made the water wine. And there was a certain nobleman, whose son was sick at Capernaum. When he heard that Jesus was come out of Judea in Galilee, he went into Him, and besought Him that He would come down and heal his son: for he was at the point of death. Then Jesus said unto him, Except ye see signs and wonders, ye will not believe. The nobleman saith unto Him, Sir, come down ere my child die. Jesus saith unto him, Go thy way; thy son liveth. And the man believed the word that Jesus had spoken unto him, and he went his way. And as he was now going down, his servants met him, and told him, saying, Thy son liveth. Then enquired he of them the hour when he began to amend. And they said unto him, yesterday at the seventh hour the fever left him. So the father knew that it was at the same hour in which Jesus said unto him, Thy son liveth: and himself believed, and his whole house.

The first manifestation of Jesus in our lives is enrichment, and there is a joyousness about that experience — a sort of "Vision splendid" — that makes us long to abide in its beauty. We have tasted and seen that the Lord is good. We have felt the wonder of the transformation of the unstable water of our nature ("Unstable as water, thou shalt not excel . . . ."[1]) — into wine — a vitalizing of our whole existence that gives new meaning to our life. Oh, to rest in this knowledge — enriched, cleansed, radiant! Oh, to do nothing to break this beauty — nothing to spoil the sweetness of this wine!

But this tarrying in an exultant mood of individual enrichment may not be. "Home" is social in its connotation. "Our Father" implies *other* children. Individual rapture and wedding festivities have to give way to the daily round with its insistent demands and duties that link our lives with others. Heaven is not yet. "Newness of life" has to be nurtured in a mortal body, subject to all the changes and disharmonies that are part of a physical world. In fact, these are the very tensions that will promote spiritual growth. As members of His family we have responsibilities of sharing and service. Sorrow and suffering, the wear and tear of daily living — these no less than joy — must test the reality of our first glad vision.

The Need for Trust

The growing soul must now pass into its second stage of development — a period of trial which is intended to promote trust. We have to learn how hard, and yet how wondrous it is to obey when God seems to have withdrawn Himself entirely from our lives.

In the "Healing of the Nobleman's Son," we see a man with a heart full of sorrow and fear — despite the enviable circumstances of birth and position that "nobleman" implies. He comes to Jesus to obtain health for his son and relief from his own anguish. And lo! this lukewarm, self-absorbed approach

[1]Gen. 49:4.

to the Savior — so weak that it is not worthy to be called "faith" — is transformed into an active belief in a Person who at first seemed to rebuff him, to ignore even his imploring invitation to come to his home and save his child, and yet who spoke the word of power which gave life more abundant than he had dreamed of receiving — not merely to his sick son, but to his entire household!

Crucial Testing

It is not possible to read this profound Sign without echoing Newman's words, "O Wisest Love!"[1] We stand, as we read, in the Presence of One who knows that if enrichment is to permeate and transform our lives, faith must follow hard upon vision, and our promise to obey in "whatsoever He saith" must be put to the test. We have to learn the hard, sweet lesson of trust. In no other way can illumination become a permanent beacon in our lives. Every family has its Mt. Moriah — its place of crucial testing — where the decisive victory of faith must be won. Sometimes we are led up that mount of testing through the failure of parents, or of children, to live up to ideals of a Christian home, because the allurements of the "far country" of the Prodigal are more to their liking than the wholesome formative disciplines and fellowship of family life; sometimes through that cold "elder brother" selfishness that stays at home to claim and receive, yet refusing to share; sometimes through the sickness of loved ones or in an untimely death. We know that vision and wine alike fail in that "midnight hour." Yet it is in that "Dark Night of the Soul" that faith is born, and like Abraham's, it is counted unto us for righteousness.

Thus it is that every growing soul sees the pattern of its growth in the experience of the nobleman of Cana. Sorrow

[1] "Praise to the Holiest in the height,
And in the depth be praise!"

enters our home or our life, and we turn to Jesus, perhaps as a last resort. We have heard of Him and of what He has done for others, and, half-hoping, half-doubting, we seek His aid. But so imperfect is our knowledge of Him that we actually expect Him to handle our problem in our way. We expect visible sympathy and help, and we find Jesus apparently indifferent to our need. Instead of doing something for us instantly, He speaks seemingly irrelevant words about a type of faith that thrives only on signs and wonders and spectacular display. This is not what we had expected. Does he care nothing about our heartbreak? Has He even heard our plea for help? We break in with a cry of anguish, "Sir, come down ere my child die!"

Our need, our need, our need! That is our one concern. We have sought Jesus not to learn of Him, but to use Him, and He appears unmoved by our suffering. He refuses to come back with us to the scene of anguish. He calmly tells us to go home, as though our child at the point of death were a mere figment of our imagination. "Go thy way; thy son liveth."

His Way — Not Ours

How can our finite minds grasp His dealings with us? How can we see that His very refusal to do things our way — a point that He made quite clear to His mother in the first Sign and which He makes equally clear to the nobleman in this second Sign — is really the lesson of paramount importance in the spiritual life. His way, His will, can never be bent to our way, our will. His method is the only way in every need. We see only one sick child; He sees a whole family lacking the abundant life that He came to bestow. He has no partial healing to offer. A family is a unit, whole — and healing means wholeness. Dumb with grief, perplexed by His method, we stand before Him. Then suddenly the Word that was made flesh invades our being. Our point of interest shifts. The

29

Savior becomes our chief concern. Our eyes are opened; the windows of our souls are enlarged. Those confident words — thrice recorded, and spoken with such calm power — assure us that this Sign is a manifestation of life, not death. There is no "death" in the vocabulary of God. Read the story again and note the startling contrast between the human and the divine: "sick," "on the point of death," "ere my child die" — these are words in our human vocabulary. "Thy son liveth! Thy son liveth! Thy son liveth!" That is the divine reiteration of truth — so divine and so true that even the servants beyond range of physical hearing catch the living accents and greet their master on his return with the ringing triumph of the Savior's words!

The Meaning of Faith

What is this faith, this trust, this quality of soul that even in the face of sin and suffering and decay and death gives us power to go on our way strong in the confidence that "Thy son liveth" is God's pronouncement of truth? The eleventh chapter of Hebrews is a magnificent outpouring of the reality of faith — a hymn of illumination and instruction which the Holy Spirit caused to be written for our learning, and which everyone who comes to Jesus earnestly seeking newness of life must "read, mark, learn, and inwardly digest."[1] The great truths set forth in that chapter show us a power that will help us meet victoriously anything and everything that life brings; that will sustain us through well-nigh impossible tasks and situations; and will give vision and value to every moment of our lives. And the more we study this "substance," this "evidence," this "title-deed," this "irrefutable proof," this "organ of spiritual touch," this "rope," this "root,"[2] striving to lay hold on the reality that transcends scholarly phrase

[1]From the Collect for the 2nd Sunday in Advent from *The Book of Common Prayer*
[2]All words used to translate or define "faith."

and inspired diction — the more surely do we know that the foundation of faith is the Rock of Ages — the uttered Word of the Father — the living Jesus, "the same yesterday, and today, and forever."[1]

I remember vividly my first serious thinking about faith, this whole tremendous problem of learning to trust. At a Harvest Festival service in Jamaica, during a season of unusual drought, we were singing that lovely hymn of praise by Anna Barbauld which begins:

> Praise to God, immortal praise,
> For the love that crowns our day.

Then because of the severity of the drought, the three additional stanzas (a paraphrase of Habakkuk 3:17,18) were ordered to be sung. I was joining in the words somewhat heedlessly, intent on tune rather than meaning, when suddenly I stopped. I knew that I did not mean what I was singing. Could I possibly love God if Mother and Father and home and friends and food and clothing and *everything* were taken away? To my child mind the vivid picture of desolation portrayed in the hymn meant that there would be nothing left for which I could give thanks. How far removed was this limited conception of Reality from St. Francis of Assisi's "My God and my All!" My faith was still in the crude, childish barter-stage of Jacob's. But the soul "wakes and grows" even as a child does, and now I know that the words,

> And when every blessing's flown,
> Love Thee for Thyself alone,

are the highest utterance of faith. In the truest sense, the withdrawal of *every* blessing is an impossibility, for God Himself is our eternal Beatitude, our eternal Blessing.

---

[1]Heb. 13:8.

31

Developing Faith

How can we have faith? Do we play any part in the development of this quality of soul, this manifestation of spiritual energy, the tiniest seed of which will bring about results that baffle human understanding? When Jesus spoke of unlimited forgiveness, His disciples, feeling utterly inadequate even to approach the reaches of divine compassion which His words opened up to them, could only turn to Him and say, "Increase our faith." And certainly He who is Author and Finisher is also the only Increaser; so like the disciples, we must turn to Him. But He does not leave us in doubt as to the part we must play in making that increase possible. In His inimitable way He answered their prayer by holding up to them a picture illustrating living faith as a source of victory and blessing. That is His gift. He then gave them the parable of the Unprofitable Servants for their instruction:

> And the apostles said unto the Lord, Increase our faith. And the Lord said, If ye had faith as a grain of mustard seed, ye might say unto this sycamine tree, Be thou plucked up by the root, and be thou planted in the sea; and it should obey you. But which of you, having a servant plowing or feeding cattle, will say unto him by and by, when he is come from the field, Go and sit down to meat? And will not rather say unto him, Make ready wherewith I may sup, and gird thyself and serve me, till I have eaten and drunken; and afterward thou shalt eat and drink? Doth he thank that servant because he did the things that were commanded him? I trow not. So likewise ye, when ye shall have done all those things which are commanded you, say, We are unprofitable servants: we have done that which was our duty to do.

He seems to say, "Look at this picture of faith. Feast your eyes upon it. Desire it with your whole heart, and then follow these instructions. Put God first. Wait upon Him in loving service, even as it is the duty of a servant to meet his master's need before his own."

Praise

Here is the essential approach to the spiritual life which Jesus had stressed from the start. The first and greatest fact is the priority of God. "Hallowed be Thy name"! Evelyn Underhill in *Abba* gives this illuminating interpretation of this phrase from the Model Prayer: "selfless adoration, awestruck worship as the ruling temper of our life and all we do."[1] That is the atmosphere in which faith is nurtured, and our business is to create that atmosphere, by the daily exercise of praise and thanksgiving. If we would learn to trust, praise must become the keynote of our life. The word "praise" originally meant "the irradiation of a luminous body." What an inspired root! When we praise God therefore, we offer ourselves as living reflectors through whom the Light of the World may diffuse His glory upon others. To praise God "morning, evening, noon, and night" is to carry out the commission which Jesus gave to each one of us when He assigned us to our place in His "rescuing system": "Ye are the light of the world."

I know of no richer source of books of praise than the Psalms, our various church hymnals, and the writings of the saints. I have never forgotten the impression made upon me when I first read the fourth paragraph in the first chapter of *The Confessions of Saint Augustine.* The sheer wonder of it held me spellbound. The ecstatic double superlative with which the outburst begins — then phrase after phrase tumbling over one another as he seeks to express in terms of startling paradox the wonder of the Inexpressible: "Most highest, most good, most potent, most omnipotent; most merciful, yet most just; most hidden, yet most present; most beautiful, yet most strong . . . ."[2] I forced myself to go on, only to turn back again and again to

---

[1] Evelyn Underhill, *Abba* (London: Longmans, Green and Co., 1940), p. 6

[2] *The Confessions of St. Augustine* (Tr. E. B. Pusey, No. 200, Everyman's Library Edition; New York: E. P. Dutton & Co., 1907), Book I, p. 3. Used by permission.

steep myself in the Immensity Whom Augustine was trying to bind in the swaddling bands of human language, yet confessing even while he tried — master rhetorician though he was — the futility of his best efforts: "And what have I now said, my God, my life, my holy joy? or what says any man when he speaks of Thee?"[1] This paragraph comes to my lips every morning when I awaken, and forms a regular part of my ascription of praise.

St. Francis of Assisi's all-comprehensive exclamation, "My God and my All!" and the opening stanza of his well-known "Canticle of the Sun" are also invaluable gems of praise. These are surpassed (so it seems to me) only by the song of the "Worship of the Lamb" by elders and angels and creatures in the book of *Revelation*[2] — and the magnificent *Te Deum* — to me the superb "Hallelujah Chorus" of all time.[3]

Keep a loose-leaf notebook. Set off one section for ascriptions of praise. Then regularly, from your devotional reading, write down any outpouring of praise that especially appeals to you. Use them frequently until they become such a part of you that they rise spontaneously to your lips in time of need — or when your heart is glad just because God is!

Thanksgiving

The second aid in deepening our faith is thanksgiving. We praise God for Himself. We thank Him for what He does for us. A plan that has helped me is to take the "General Thanksgiving" and make it an act of personal gratitude to God. After this it takes on a deeper meaning when said in unison with His family. Each soul should thank God daily (at least) for preservation, redemption, sanctification, means of grace, and hope of glory. Thankfulness is an attitude of mind that needs ceaseless cultivation.

[1]*Loc. cit.*
[2]Rev. 4:11; 5:12,13
[3]See Appendices for texts mentioned here.

Archbishop Fenelon in *Christian Perfection* asks a searching question that it would be well for each child of God to consider: "Would we want to be treated by a son, or even by a servant, as we treat God?"[1] Most of us take God's blessings for granted. We thank Him mainly for His answers to our prayers and for personal benefits. But the thanksgiving that exalts a soul, that kills depression, that makes religion real and vital, and increases our faith in God is that which we offer for those bountiful gifts which He offers alike to all: His mercy, His love, His inestimable gift of Jesus. How often do we pause to thank Jesus for His incarnation, His ministry, His compassion, His teaching, His sufferings, His institution of the Lord's Supper? How often do we thank the Holy Spirit for His brooding on the face of the waters and bringing our universe to birth, for His cleansing and quickening power in our hearts, for His indwelling and sanctification of His new creation, the holy Church throughout the world?[2]

A very helpful type of thanksgiving that I use is based on the invocations and petitions of the collects for the church year — for example, that familiar "Collect for Aid against Perils," one of the tenderest prayers of evensong.

> Lighten our darkness, we beseech thee, O Lord;
> and by thy great mercy defend us from all
> perils and dangers of this night; for the love of
> thy only Son, our Saviour, Jesus Christ. Amen.[3]

The invocation of a collect is founded on some part of God's revelation of Himself in the Bible. "Lighten our darkness." Let us turn that petition into a thanksgiving: "I thank thee, O Lord, that thou dost lighten my darkness, and, by thy great mercy, dost defend me from all the perils and dangers of this

---

[1] Francois de Salignac de la Mothe Fenelon, *Christian Perfection.* Ed. by Charles F. Whiston; tr. by Mildred Whitney Stillman (New York:Harper & Bros., 1947), Letter 30, p. 116.

[2] From the *Te Deum.*

[3] Collect for Evening Prayer from *The Book of Common Prayer.*

night." Make your own collection of individual thanksgivings from your favorite prayers, your Bible reading, and your hymns.

Necessity of New Faith

Faith, then, the faculty which grasps the unseen, may be developed by praise and thanksgiving—the first important step for those who would walk in newness of life. There are other important aspects of prayer which will come later. But this is an imperative start. Prayer has been called the "organ of spiritual touch," and most of us, like the unfortunate man in Luke 6:6, 10, go through life with a withered right hand. No matter how weak that organ of touch seems, stretch it forth, as bravely as the nobleman of Cana stretched forth his. Shift from self-interest to the priority of God, and take Jesus at His word. That hand, however limp, outstretched to Him will daily grow stronger. His vital life will flow into it, quickening the flabby muscles and putting new vigor into the hardened veins. The unseen things of which we are now so slightly aware will become real. From strength to strength we shall climb the steep ascent of whatever Mount of Testing lies before us, praising and thanking our loving Father and Savior for Himself and for His great gift of life. Then, if our faith fail not, in a moment of glad certainty, we shall know Him in whom we have believed.

Look again at the healing of the Nobleman's son. "Jesus saith unto him, Go thy way; thy son liveth. And the man *believed the word* that Jesus had spoken unto him, and he went his way."[1]

[1] John 4:50.

36

Chapter Three

Restoration

John 5:1-15

(The Healing of the Impotent Man)

After this there was a feast of the Jews; and Jesus went up to Jerusalem. Now there is at Jerusalem by the sheep market a pool, which is called in the Hebrew tongue Bethesda, having five porches. In these lay a great multitude of impotent folk, of blind, halt, withered, waiting for the moving of the water. For an angel went down at a certain season into the pool, and troubled the water: whosoever then first after the troubling of the water stepped in was made whole of whatsoever disease he had. And a certain man was there, which had an infirmity thirty and eight years. When Jesus saw him lie, and knew that he had been now a long time *in that case,* He saith unto him, Wilt thou be made whole? The impotent man answered Him, Sir, I have no man, when the water is troubled, to put me into the pool: but while I am coming, another steppeth down before me. Jesus saith unto him, Rise, take up thy bed, and walk. And immediately the man was made whole, and took up his bed, and walked: and on the same day was the sabbath. The Jews therefore said unto him that was cured, It is the sabbath day: it is not lawful for thee to carry *thy* bed. He answered them, He that made me whole, the same said unto me, Take up thy bed, and walk. Then asked they him, What man is that which said unto thee, Take up thy bed, and walk? And he that was healed wist not who it was: for Jesus had conveyed Himself away, a multitude being in *that* place. Afterward Jesus findeth him in the temple, and said unto him, Behold, thou art made whole: sin no more, lest a worse thing come unto thee. The man departed, and told the Jews that it was Jesus, which had made him whole.

Newness of life is an activity of soul—a pressing ever upward and onward. Jesus calls us to be hardy mountain climbers who will steadfastly ascend the hill of the Lord until we ultimately dwell in His holy place. Throughout the ages this idea of ascent has led great teachers of the spiritual life to see a ladder as a symbol of the upward climb of the soul. Some have arranged their instructions in simple and vivid ladder-form, one step at a time, so that souls under their direction might climb gradually—"Heaven is not reached by a single bound"—and make each step sure before going on to the next. Dr. E. Stanley Jones used the ladder method very effectively.[1] And the ladder does have deep scriptural significance. Men who have pondered the great stories of Genesis see in Jacob's ladder a foreshadowing of Jesus—the living Way between God and man—His descent to us making possible our ascent to Him. It is therefore helpful to visualize these Signs of the Fourth Gospel as seven steps in our ascent to God, in and through Jesus. The first step brought us a glad consciousness of general enrichment; the second taught the hard, sweet lesson of trust, and gave us our first spiritual assignment, the daily exercise of praise and thanksgiving. And now, in the strength of our Savior, we must press on to the third step and there undergo the great experience of restoration.

Meaning of Restoration

The word "restoration" is in itself a description of what is to happen to us as we study this third Sign, "The Healing of the Impotent Man." We are restored, "put back into the original form" in which our heavenly Father created us. That divine likeness, "His own image," which we have defaced and darkened, has to be restored to its original brightness and beauty, so that it may shine forth in our lives. Our

[1]E. Stanley Jones, *Abundant Living* (New York: Abingdon-Cokesbury Press, 1942), pp. 289,294.

bodies in which He chooses to dwell must be made whole; our misused powers must be redirected; our dormant capabilities must be awakened; and all the gracious inflow of new life must be channeled into the twin activities of love and service for which we were created.

So Jesus, the Good Shepherd, intent on seeking and saving, finds us at our Pool of Bethesda—whatever state of weakness that may represent in each individual life. What a picture of living death is that crowd of helpless human beings, "withered and waiting," beside the Pool of Mercy year after year, for "Bethesda" means "House of Mercy." Yet like bright-winged Hope amid the evils in Pandora's box, there is a note of expectancy in the word "waiting," a hint that help is at hand. We have no time to sit, much less to lie, at ease, if we are to be enrolled in His glorious company of disciples and co-workers. Ineffectual men and women cannot be about their Father's business. Man was not made to be a failure, for, as a child of God, some attributes of his Father—power, purity, perfection—are latent in him. To "be a man" implies conduct that is in keeping with the Divine Image in which man was created.

Jesus calls us to be men. The Bible abounds in ringing, authoritative summons uttered by God to men who seemed weak and incompetent, but whom God had planned to use. We cannot read those vibrant commands—despite the centuries that have elapsed since they were sounded—without a quickening of the pulse and a desire to be up and doing. "Go from your country and your kindred and your father's house...."[1] "Come, and I will send you...."[2] "Go, prophesy to my people Israel."[3] "Gird up your loins, and arise."[4]

[1] Gen. 12:1.
[2] Exod. 3:10.
[3] Amos 7:15.
[4] Jer. 1:17.

"Stand upon your feet, and I will speak with you."[1] "Arise, take up your bed, and walk."[2]

The story of Jeremiah is an antidote for diffident moods. Sensitive, timid, utterly inadequate in physique and temperament to be God's messenger, he receives the astounding, and seemingly ironic, announcement that God intends to make of him "a fortified city, an iron pillar and bronze walls...."[3] And lo! the Lord puts forth His hand and touches Jeremiah's mouth, and the young man's agony of inability is changed into indomitable courage.

Franz Werfel, in his classic portrayal of Jeremiah, brings out the fact that the command which God keeps reiterating to the prophet is "Go," and he helps us to see the heroic blotting out of self that it involved: "The short word 'go' suddenly swarmed with new meanings.... Take new burdens upon thyself! Do that which hitherto has been uncongenial to thee, that which is hardest for thee, that which torments thee most and inspires thee with fear!"[4] And yet such transformation takes place when Jeremiah's weakness becomes a receptacle for the power of the Holy Spirit that a new vocabulary is found on the lips of one whose first response to God was the despairing cry, "Ah, Lord God! behold I cannot speak: for I am a child."[5]

What Wholeness Involves

Even so does Jesus call us from our pool of frustration— whatever it may be—to arise and share in that wholeness of life which is fulness of joy—the joy of working with Him in His great task of re-creation. He sees our condition, hears

[1]Ezek. 2:1.
[2]John 5:8. (Revised Standard Version of Holy Bible).
[3]Jer. 1:18.
[4]Franz, Werfel, *Hearken Unto the Voice* (New York: The Viking Press, Inc., 1938), tr. by Moray Firth, pp. 137, 139.
[5]Jer. 1:6.

our confession of utter helplessness, then quietly asks us if we want to assume the responsibilities and burdens of a life of service. The question is a searching one. Are we really weary of our wasted years, or have we become so accustomed to inactivity that we are finding a certain morbid satisfaction in it? If we want restoration—and it is never thrust upon us; it has to be our own choice—then the Pool of Bethesda knows us no more. The temple now becomes our place of meeting with the Master. Henceforth we live "not to be ministered unto, but to minister." "Arise, take up your bed and walk."[1]

Every life and every home is the richer for such restoration. We all know how easy it is to give in to physical weariness, to become absorbed and frustrated by defeat and failure. The impotent man at Bethesda's Pool is not of the noble army of genuine sufferers—men and women with crippled, diseased, pain-wracked bodies whose physical condition is the result neither of sin nor of temperament and whose affliction, like the afflictions of the saints throughout the ages, will be understood only when the whole mystifying problem of pain is made clear, and sin and evil and death are no more. History is full of gallant sufferers whose bodies have housed such wholeness of soul that the service they rendered to all who knew them far outmeasured any that they received. But almost every home shelters a neurotic member, the man or woman who can talk of nothing but his ailments, and who has become such a prey to negative thinking that his presence is like a miasma, an unhealthy atmosphere in which no constructive thought can thrive. These are the weak, the unable ones, whose infirmities St. Paul says we, the strong, the able, the restored, ought to bear.[2] Moffatt gives a most illuminating translation: "We who are strong ought to bear the burdens

[1]John 5:8.
[2]Rom. 15:1.

42

that the weak make for themselves and us.''[1] Educational
psychology helps us to detect this neurotic pattern in its
first showings—when very small children begin to feel sick
and run up a temperature as an escape measure, as soon as
they face an unpleasant or difficult task.

Facing Difficulties

Restoration, however, means the putting away of all escape
measures and the putting on of what the late Dr. Halford E.
Luccock, of Yale University Divinity School, called "crazy
logic." He gave us, it seems to me, an unerring measuring
rod for our neurotic tendencies, when he tells us to watch
our use of the connective "therefore." The early Church
used it "crazily."

> Persecution and imprisonment rampant; therefore
> they kept right on doing what brought on the persecution.
> ...the caution and strategy with which we are so pain-
> fully familiar..., would have it read like this: "Violent
> persecution arose. Therefore they all lay low and ceased
> preaching until the storm blew over." ...But these naive
> disciples had a "crazy" logic. It was apostolic; and it
> was divine. Difficulty, persecution, death, if they went
> on preaching. *Therefore,* they went on preaching....[2]

What a powerful connective with which to break the spell
of impotence! It is difficult to take up the duties that God lays
upon us. Therefore, we arise and take them up and perform
them in His strength. The impotent man at Bethesda had that
"crazy logic." He had lain in a hopeless and helpless condition of body and mind for thirty-eight years. Every year
for many years (we don't know how many) he had dragged
himself to the edge of the pool, only to be pushed aside by some

[1]From: *The Bible: A New Translation,* by James Moffatt, copyrighted by Harper &
Bros., 1935. Used by permission.
[2]Halford E. Luccock, *The Acts of the Apostles in Present-Day Preaching.* Copyrighted by
Harper & Bros., 1942. Used by permission. (Itals. mine, Ed.)

stronger sufferer—and had dragged himself back to his mat to wait another twelve months! Suddenly one day—perhaps just after such a frustrated attempt to reach the healing waters—a stranger comes up to him, asks him if he wishes to be well, then tells him to get up and take up his bed and walk! No one had ever told him to do such an impossible thing. *Therefore,* he does it! There is sheer heroism here. We expect him to say, "Wait a minute, Sir! Don't you think you are going a little too fast! For thirty-eight years I've hardly been able to sit up, much less stand!"—and so on, in that weak, self-pitying strain. But, no! He gets up instantly, takes up his bed, and walks. His action does savor of "crazy" apostolic courage and confidence! "Whatsoever He saith unto you...." Therefore we do it!

We know of course that the source of this exhilarating power is Jesus—His radiant, vital personality, His sure tone of command. The word He uses, "Arise!" is in itself a healing—a coming to grips with reality—a standing tall, an awakening. It is the word that indicates the restoration of the Prodigal. "I will arise,"[1] an expression of the invisible moral healing that had taken place in his nature before the outward visible action of going to his father could take place. There is a joyous note in Moffatt's translation, "I will be up and off to my father," but I am glad that the translators of the Revised Standard Version have kept "I will arise" before the words "and go." I rather wish that they had combined the two: "I will arise and be up and off to my father!" for there is an ecstasy in the "up and off," a sort of "everyone-suddenly-burst-out-singing" kind of mood that instinctively makes one glad for the waiting father, and gives an assurance that the son will not change his mind—in fact, a feeling that he will run all the way home!

Inward Healing

Thus restoration takes place in all of us at the command, "Arise!" There is a straightening up of our moral nature, no matter how low it has fallen. There is an air of gladness as of a captive leaping "to loose his chains."

But just as "earth's crammed with heaven,"[1] so is this amazing Sign crammed with lessons. Let us reflect on the question, "Wilt thou be made whole?" Archbishop John Henry Bernard in his commentary on this Gospel, says that the Greek conveys a simple question such as, "Would you like to be well?" and that no conscious effort of will to co-operate in the healing need be implied. And yet the "wilt" has always turned my thought to the pre-Advent prayer: "Stir up, we beseech thee, O Lord, the wills of thy faithful people." We who want so sincerely to be "faithful," know only too well that weakness of will lies at the root of our feeble spiritual life. To all of us, time and again, John Drinkwater's plea has become a personal cry:

> But, Lord, the will—there lies our bitter need;
> Give us to build above the deep intent
> The deed, the deed.[2]

So often we have been aroused, have stood upon our feet, have even gone so far as to show a spurt of activity in our Father's business—and then our will weakens, and we settle back into our old complacency, our comfortable inactivity, yearning again for the attention and coddling that "unable-ness" too often brings. Well do we remember Joe, the fat boy in *Pickwick Papers!* No matter how vigorously or how frequently he was aroused, he inevitably fell asleep again. There must be an effort of will if spiritual growth is to con-tinue. And this moment-by-moment business of keeping the laggard will stirred up is the obligation that restoration lays upon us.

[1] Elizabeth Barnett Browning in *Aurora Lee.*
> Earth's crammed with heaven,
> And every common bush afire with God.
> But only he who sees takes off his shoes.
> The rest sit around it and pick blackberries.

[2] John Drinkwater, *Poems 1908-1919* (New York: Curtis Brown, Ltd., 1919). Used by permission.

45

Ordered Living

Our inward wholeness must be expressed in action. We have to arise and "walk in newness of life."[1] Our lives must be ordered, so that they may be fruitful. The joyous exercises of praise and thanksgiving must now be expanded into a more exacting rule of life. There must be an earnest consecration of our personality and talents—no matter how inadequate they seem—for the service of others. Bible reading now becomes a daily "must." Every morning we are under obligation to turn to our Captain for orders. We have to drink deep of the living water of the "Well of Bethlehem" so that we may be strong to serve. We need a definite plan of daily Bible readings conjoined with others in our fellowship or our denomination, if possible. There is an unmistakeable sense of corporate uplift when all the members of a great fellowship read the same portion of Scripture daily. But if we feel we can do more than that first suggested "mile," then let us read some extra portion. *The Bible for Today,* edited by John Stirling and published by the Oxford University Press, is one of the finest adventures in Bible reading that I know. The brief prefaces to each section are pertinent to our need, and the whole inspired arrangement from Genesis to Revelation is an unfolding of God's majestic plan of holiness for mankind—beginning with Israel, and embracing the whole earth. I have loved the Bible from childhood, have read it often, as they say, "from cover to cover," and yet when about six years ago I was given a copy of *The Bible for Today,* I experienced something of the breathless wonder of discovery and felt as never before the great wind that "blows through Ezekiel and John." But whatever plan of reading we follow, the important thing is to read, and from our reading to store in our hearts at least a verse or a phrase to live with throughout the day and to practice in our daily life, for, as Luther warns, we do not go to the Bible to read God's commands, but to hear God commanding!

[1] Romans 6:4

The Problem of Sin

But we cannot leave this Sign without considering what is perhaps its most vital lesson—the part that forgiveness plays in restoration. Our Lord finds the restored man in the Temple and gives him an injunction that has an almost ominous sound: "Sin no more, lest a worse thing come unto thee."[1] Restoration involves looking with enlightened eyes on the stark fact of sin—a fact which each of us has to face honestly and humbly if restoration is to be permanent. The presence and power of sin is hinted at or expressed in each of St. John's seven Signs: in the waterpots for purification, in the first; in the sickness in the nobleman's home, in the second; and in our Lord's frank warning of the possibility of a relapse, in the third. At the Pool of Bethesda the "kind but searching eyes" of Jesus saw the sin that lay behind thirty-eight wasted years. Therefore the man knew that healing had begun with forgiveness. The rapture of his arising and the thankfulness that hurried him to the Temple speak eloquently of a loosening of double chains—the heart from sin, the body from infirmity. Jesus took sin seriously and waged an uncompromising warfare with it for our sakes. How tenderly true are the lines in one of our best-loved children's hymns:

> He died that we might be forgiven,
> He died to make us good.

In *Christian Doctrine*, Dr. J. S. Whale has a penetrating chapter on "Man and His Sin." He shows that the questions of the nature of sin and how one may get rid of it are fundamental in the teaching of Christianity. He points out the agonizing need of forgiveness in the lives of those who have really surrendered to Jesus, naming a few—Paul, Bunyan, Luther, Chesterton. So real was sin to these men that

[1]John 5:14.

Chesterton says that he went over to the Church of Rome to get rid of his sins, and Luther was driven away from the Papacy to get rid of his! Dr. Whale defines sin as "moral evil seen in its relation to God."[1] In other words, sin is not our private concern; God is involved; and, furthermore, getting rid of sin depends on God's graciousness alone; and He shows us the only way of restoration—Jesus.

It is not surprising, therefore, that Jesus stressed forgiveness in every phase of his ministry and gave it the first place in His works of healing. This fundamental need of the soul has not changed. If we are honest with ourselves, we know that bread for our bodies and forgiveness for our souls are still where Jesus placed them—first on the list of human needs.

Divine Forgiveness

The world has made great strides in material knowledge since that far-off Sabbath Day when the Lord of Life, who gives life to whomsoever He chooses, paused at the Pool of Bethesda, forgave an impotent man his sins, and bade him arise and sin no more. Advance in science has helped us to understand more clearly the natural laws governing the universe in which we live; psychiatrists have given us clearer insight into certain aspects of human nature, enabling us (it is to be hoped) to live more happily with ourselves, our neighbors, and our world; biologists have freed us from certain fears by a fuller revelation of how our bodies function, and of the part played by glands, emotions, and food in the reactions of this baffling human "thinking machine." Everything that man can do to help us to build aright and to order wisely the lower story of our House of Physical Life has been done. Yet, where the wholeness of the personality and the abundant

---

[1] J. S. Whale, *Christian Doctrine* (London: Cambridge University Press, 1942), p. 12.

life of the soul are concerned, Jesus, for "yesterday, and today, and forever," has spoken the last and only authoritative word. It remains for us, under the guidance of the Holy Spirit, to grasp and appropriate His teaching and allow it to transform our lives.

The "transfer" brought about by the psychiatrist, when he helps a patient to unburden his mind, is not the "wholeness" that Jesus offers, for the perfect and permanent "transfer" of guilt lies in forgiveness, which God alone can give. Sunday after Sunday the Church holds out to us this certain way of wholeness: "If we confess our sins, He is faithful and just to forgive us our sins and to cleanse us from all unrighteousness."[1] To come to Him and know that we are forgiven; to see the glorious vistas of "a godly, righteous, and sober life" stretching before us; to "walk in newness of life,"[2] rejoicing in the exhilaration of the "glad, confident morning" that wholeness brings—this is the wonder and blessedness of restoration—and it comes to us solely from the full, free, overflowing love of our Heavenly Father: "Behold, what manner of love the Father hath bestowed upon us!"[3]

[1] I John 1:9. KJV.
[2] Phrases are taken from General Confession, Book of Common Prayer.
[3] I John 3:1. KJV.

Chapter Four

Sustenance

John 6:1-14
The Feeding of the Five Thousand

After these things Jesus went over the sea of Galilee, which is *the sea* of Tiberias. And a great multitude followed Him, because they saw His miracles which He did on them that were diseased. And Jesus went up into a mountain, and there He sat with His disciples. And the passover, a feast of the Jews, was nigh. When Jesus then lifted up *His* eyes, and saw a great company come unto Him, He saith unto Philip, Whence shall we buy bread, that these may eat? And this He said to prove Him: for He Himself knew what He would do. Philip answered Him, Two hundred pennyworth of bread is not sufficient for them, that every one of them may take a little. One of His disciples, Andrew, Simon Peter's brother, saith unto Him, There is a lad here which hath five barley loaves, and two small fishes: but what are they among so many? And Jesus said, Make the men sit down. Now there was much grass in the place. So the men sat down, in number about five thousand. And Jesus took the loaves; and when He had given thanks, He distributed to the disciples, and the disciples to them that were set down; and likewise of the fishes as much as they would. When they were filled, He said unto His disciples, Gather up the fragments that remain, that nothing be lost. Therefore they gathered *them* together, and filled twelve baskets with the fragments of the five barley loaves, which remained over and above unto them that had eaten. Then those men, when they had seen the miracle that Jesus did, said, This is of a truth that prophet that should come into the world.

New birth, learning to trust, restoration—so the pattern of "newness of life" grows. He who restored us and bade us sin no more gives us power to carry out that command, and that power is sustenance—food—meat and drink—unified as "bread" in the "Feeding of the Five Thousand." In this fourth and central Sign, we see Jesus manifesting His glory by revealing Himself as the support of our life—the living, true, and heavenly Bread—the great Gift of the Father to all His children. This step is indeed a standing on holy ground, and our approach should be made in the mood of "selfless adoration, awestruck worship," which Evelyn Underhill urges us to cultivate in our hallowing of His Name.

Events Preceding Sign

Let us go in thought to the scene of this Sign. It is the only miracle recorded by all four evangelists; and what an unforgettable experience it must have been! A hungry crowd sitting in orderly fasion at the feet of the Lord of Life, expecting to be fed! It took place at the close of the second period of His Galilean ministry. The Twelve had just returned from their first mission—a sort of trial test to see what they could do on their own—like fledglings being forced from the nest to try their wings. There is an austerity about the manner in which Christ sent them that emphasizes the lesson taught in the third Sign—that Jesus wants men, not weaklings. They are given two commands: to preach the kingdom and to heal the sick—the Reign of God and wholeness—the same twin concerns for which He enlists us today. He seemed to be deliberately making things difficult for them. No going forth as a confident team of twelve, but in twos, so that individual talents and abilities might find expression; no change of clothing; no money; no food; no rooms reserved in advance— what a lesson in learning to trust! Can they preach and teach and heal so effectively and so joyously that the door of every home will be flung wide to them, and their needs abundantly supplied by grateful people who have benefited by their free and loving ministry? Do we feel embarrassed as we read?

And now they have returned—and what a lot they have to talk over with Him! But the excitement of their mission is sobered by the tidings, noised about all over the countryside, that John the Baptist has been beheaded. More sinister still is the rumor that the doings of Jesus have convinced the uneasy Herod that the murder of John has been in vain, for he sees the Baptist risen in the person of Jesus and showing forth even mightier works than before his execution. Jesus knows this means that He is now the object of the open enmity of Herod's followers. So He withdraws to a quiet spot on the eastern side of the Sea of Galilee to listen to the reports of the Twelve, to plan His course of action, to get some needed rest.

But the proposed rest is broken. Crowds intrude upon His privacy and His sorrow. Joined by other travelers going to Jerusalem to the approaching Passover, they follow Him to the scene of His retirement, and when He sees them thronging to the base of the hill to which He has withdrawn with His disciples, He forgets His own need and welcomes this opportunity to preach and to heal; and so He teaches and restores all day, until eventide comes, and the scene is set for the Sign—a weary, hungry crowd with no provisions, confronting the Lord of Life, their source of plenty.

With the same quiet assurance that makes Jesus the dominating Figure in all these Signs, He gives the practical, businesslike Philip an opportunity to show his faith. Philip frankly confesses the hopelessness of the situation. Andrew, eager to help, but also seeing nothing beyond the obvious means, mentions a little lad with a ridiculously small supply— five loaves and two fishes—and supports Philip's conviction that the situation is hopeless. Human extremity! that is always the point where Jesus takes over.

"They have no wine," said His mother in the first sign. "Come down ere my child die" is the nobleman's expression indicating that all earthly help is at an end. "Sir, I have no man," declared the impotent man at Bethesda. Nothing left—but Jesus! Oh, if only Philip and Andrew could have measured up a little more royally to the Master's stature! If, after seeing the situation to which there was no human solution—insufficient money, no food shops, two fishes, five loaves, over five thousand people—they had but answered (as Dr. Marcus Dods suggests), "[Master], 'we have neither meat nor money, but we have Thee'[1]!"

The crowd sits down, hushed and expectant, for although they know it not, they are feeling a Presence who is the supply for all need. This is to be no little taste to stay the pangs of hunger until they get home, but a meal from the full, overflowing table of the Lord: "Open your mouth wide, and I will fill it"[2]!

Jesus our Spiritual Food

The Sign is staggering in its implications—God offering His very self to us for our spiritual food! Just as in the process of physical digestion natural food actually becomes a part of us by repairing damaged cells and building new ones, even so the Bread of Heaven is to be eaten, assimilated into the "inner man," this new spiritual self that is being fashioned within us as the result of new birth. But food is of little benefit if we have no desire to eat it. In its original tongue, the verb that St. John uses for "eat" in the discourse that follows this Sign is expressive of eating that results from fierce hunger. We are to hunger for Jesus as ravenously as a famished man hungers for food. A gnawing hunger and a panting thirst are the marks of the restored soul.

[1]Marcus Dods, *The Gospel of St. John* (New York: *The Expositor's Bible,* ed. by W. R. Nicoll, A. C. Armstrong and Son, 1908), Vol. I, p. 210.
[2]Ps. 81:10. RSV.

Startling language! so startling that many disciples went back from following Jesus because His words were too difficult. It is all so tremendous, so incomprehensibly divine that we cannot follow the thought of the Almighty. Yet here is our God coming to us in His most royal way! The word "bread" implies sacrifice; for the Anglo-Saxon root means "broken," and the French root "pounded," the crushing and pounding of grain, so that mankind may be nourished. But even more compelling than the idea of sacrifice is the thought of love—"so amazing, so divine"—that lies behind the giving. That He should offer Himself for us at all is the incomprehensible wonder!

> Bread of the world in mercy broken,
> Wine of the soul in mercy shed.[1]

It is not possible to sing these words at the service of Holy Communion without a sense of exultance that makes it difficult for us to remain on our knees. We want to rise and sing "Glory to God in the Highest!" It was this love without reason or limit that moved St. Augustine to cry: "What art Thou to me? In Thy pity, teach me to utter it. Or what am I to Thee that Thou demandest my love...?"[2] And Charles Wesley, in rapt contemplation of the same ineffable experience, saw the saints gazing in speechless ecstasy throughout eternity at the wonder of a crucified God—God self-given for sacrifice![3]

Purpose of Food

Thus the restored soul is led to its source of sustenance. We have been sent forth to labor in God's vineyard, and a laborer needs food. But food is offered for only one purpose—

[1] Reginald Heber.
[2] *The Confessions of St. Augustine,* op. cit., p. 3. Used by permission.
[3] Referring to the last stanza of "Love Divine, All loves excelling."

> Changed from glory into glory,
> Till in heaven we take our place,
> Till we cast our crowns before thee,
> Lost in wonder, love, and praise.

to give us strength to perform the duties that life brings, and the amount we eat should be regulated by the outlay of energy required for our work. St. Paul made it absolutely clear that an idle person forfeits his right to daily bread. The late Dr. Charles Reynolds Brown, a former Dean of the Yale University Divinity School, adapted St. Paul's statement to our twentieth century living by saying that instead of complaining about food that is set before us, we should ask ourselves the primary questions: "Am I worth feeding? Is it important that I should be kept alive? Does the world particularly need another one of my type?"[1]

Scientific research has proved that sufficient food helps, but that excess hinders, and that there is no end to the bodily ills that are brought about by overeating, as well as by undereating. To help us in this important matter of balance, the Holy Spirit gives us the virtue of temperance, another name for prudence, and called by St. Thomas Aquinas "the Virtue of the Beautiful." Temperance will help us to order all things rightly—to keep a perfect balance between the "too little" and the "too much"—the omissions and commissions that play such havoc with our spiritual growth. What a wealth of instruction lies for us in this Sign of wonder and of grace! "I am the bread of life; he that cometh to Me shall never hunger,"[2] says Jesus, as He seeks to turn our thought from the perishable food to the food that is life itself. "I am the living bread which came down from heaven: if any man eat of this bread, he shall live for ever."[3]

Main Channels of Food

"Lord, evermore give us this bread."[4] That can be our only response. Let us consider how we may obtain it. We have already undertaken the daily practice of praise and

---

[1] *The Master's Influence,* Charles Reynolds Brown (Nashville: Cokesbury Press, 1936), p. 107.
[2] John 6:35. KJV.   [3] John 6:51. KJV.   [4] John 6:34. KJV.

thanksgiving, to which has been added the exercise of daily Bible reading. Now we must order our devotional life even more deliberately, so that we may receive sustenance. There are four main channels through which this living bread comes to us. I put daily Bible reading first, because our source book of the spiritual life is the Bible, on which all reliable guide-books are based. In order to know and love and serve God, we must read His Word. But now, under the direction of the Holy Spirit, we must spend a few minutes in earnest, orderly reflection on what we read, so that we may relate to our every-day living the daily message received from our Master. This ordered thought is called meditation—a simple, but essential aspect of prayer. "Meditation consists of placing our Lord before the eyes, in the heart, and in the hands."[1] This means looking at Jesus (adoration); loving Jesus (communion) and serving Jesus (cooperation). We must now set aside ten minutes daily for this most effective exercise. All who make a regular practice of meditation testify to the enrichment and the sustaining power that it brings. "They that wait upon the Lord shall renew their strength; they shall mount up with wings as eagles; they shall run, and not be weary; and they shall walk, and not faint."[2]

Meditation

Here is a brief example of the process of meditation. Let us choose the simple request, "Lord, teach us to pray." First, picture the scene and try to see ourselves with the disciples actually watching Jesus in the act of prayer. This is Jesus "before the eyes." Then, as we keep our eyes upon Him, the compelling beauty of His person, the thought that He is ever praying for us, the wonder of his love, and any other thought about Him that the Holy Spirit may prompt, will stir our affection and kindle in our hearts a deeper love for Him.

[1]Berulle, *Oeuvres*, p.62.
[2]Isa. 40:31.

This is Jesus "in the heart." But since communion with one whom we love makes us seek to express that love in service, so we shall find ourselves asking, "Lord, what wilt Thou have me to do?"[1] If our love is sincere, it will stir up our wills to seize the suggestions that the Holy Spirit will make to us—some glad giving of ourselves for others or some determined attack on a specific defect of character or disposition. This is Jesus "in the hands." Such meditation will send us forth "strong in the power of His might," ready and willing for His sake to meet whatever the day may bring, with the confidence and courage of a co-worker with God.

Prayer

The second means by which we receive spiritual food is prayer. What is prayer? The question has almost as many answers as there are individual Christians, for everyone who is concerned with the spiritual life is concerned with prayer. Varied and rich are the contributions that have been made by individual believers and by the masters in the spiritual life. A good starting place is Luke 11:1, from which we chose our topic for meditation. The disciples, having watched Jesus praying and having seen in His act a quality and an approach so unlike anything they had ever practiced or witnessed, turned to Him and said, "Lord, teach us to pray." This instructs us that a study of prayer must begin with Jesus, the ablest and the best Teacher.

Prayer in the Old Testament

Now the first thing a good teacher does is to give his pupils a background of what is already known about the subject. Jesus therefore leads us to a wealth of material—the teaching of the Old Testament on prayer. Have we listed the things for which patriarchs, kings, prophets, and psalmists prayed?

[1]Acts 9:6.

It is a valuable exercise to test our praying by the prayers of these ancient guides: Abraham prayed for his son and his nephew; Abraham's servant asked for guidance that he might wisely carry out the commission entrusted to him by his master; Jacob came out of a great religious experience with a prayer on his lips, not knowing that his prayer to return home in peace would result in a night of agonizing wrestling by the brook Jabbok, when the process of his inner transformation would being and without which no peace could be possible for him; and so on—prayer after prayer opening up new vistas of the invisible world that is even nearer than our outstretched arm! Do we pray for our relatives—the difficult ones especially? Do we pray for guidance in our daily undertakings, in the carrying out of tasks laid upon us by family or church? Does a deep religious experience through prayer result in drastic changes in our life and in our personality? Can one wrestle with God in prayer and come out lame, yet victorious? These are indeed absorbing questions. And these early prayers lead us on to the mountaintop of prayer, where we sit humbly at the feet of the Master and ask Him to mould our findings into the perfect whole of His prayer, and to pattern our praying after His.

Pattern Prayer

Jesus answers our need by giving us a perfect prayer-pattern, the Lord's Prayer. His teaching is clear and direct. Prayer is a Father-son relationship. It is a dutiful son talking over with his Father his Father's business and the share the son has in it. The Father and His business come first: His Name, His kingdom, His will. Then follow the three great needs of the son—food, forgiveness, guidance—so that he may be fitted and sustained to set about the one concern of his life—his Father's business, and that he may glorify his Father in all that he does. Those of us who still have with us (or have had) fathers and mothers whom we love more than we can ever show in deeds or express in words, know how this revelation of prayer pulls at our heartstrings. "When Israel was a child, I loved him, and called my son out of Egypt,"[1] so that the Son might make known to the world His Father's way of life—the nature of true religion. That call of the Father shows what prayer really is. We do not need to bother too much about definitions, but we do need to pray—our very life depends upon it. We come to our Father in order to know Him better, to love Him more completely, to grow more like the pattern He has set before us in His Son and to serve Him more perfectly—the Father always first, the son's gladness and fulness of life derived from and centered in the Father.

Naturalness of Prayer

The most helpful talk I ever had on prayer was with my own father, when he was nearing the end of his pilgrimage. We were discussing some of the books on prayer that I had read, and he said: "Prayer is very simple; it is keeping at it that is difficult; but if you love, you will keep at it. When you were very young, you used to climb into my bed early in the morning, and your first question always was, 'Daddy, what are you going to do for me today?' I used to smile to myself and, as I answered you, I thought, 'She is very young, and she is still her first and only concern, but I am glad she comes to me, for her very coming and asking show that she depends upon me and knows that I have her good at heart.' Then, as you grew older, the day came when you said, 'Daddy, what did you do when you were a little boy?' And I was glad that the point of interest was shifting from self. And finally there came the day when you asked, 'Daddy, how can I grow more like you? How can I be as good as you?' Then I humbly rejoiced, because I knew that the same pattern would be reproduced in your approach to your Heavenly Father, if only you would keep on going to

[1] Hos. 11:1.

61

Him daily and talking things over with Him as you did with me. I believe that Jesus means us to come to Him as simply and as sincerely as a child comes to his father, for well He knows that if the child will keep on coming, He will lose himself—and find himself—in the Father, and eventually the Father will be all.''

Holy Communion

The third great channel through which we are fed is the ''Blessed Sacrament of His Body and Blood.'' We come to it, and the sustenance we receive gives us strength and illumination. This great Sacrament instituted by our Lord is called by several names, because it expresses a reality that no single name can hold. It is called the ''Holy Eucharist'' because it is the crown and completion of all our acts of thanksgiving. The word ''eucharist'' comes from the Greek and means ''thanksgiving.'' It is called the ''Mass'' from the Latin word *missa* meaning ''dismissed,'' because the unbaptized were dismissed before the most sacred part of the service began, and because of the sacrificial aspect of the Sacrament is emphasized. It is called ''Holy Communion'' because feeding with spiritual food is stressed. We think of the Sacrament as a means of communion with God and with one another—that indwelling which sustains and transforms. It is called the ''Lord's Supper'' because of its memorial aspect. It takes us back in thought to that supper in the upper room on the night of His betrayal, when He told us, ''Do this in remembrance of Me.'' Thus thanksgiving, sacrifice, sustenance, memorial are all embodied in this Sacrament which Jesus instituted for the purpose of drawing us to Him in the most intimate and perfect union. It is the tragedy of Christendom that this plan of His, to make us one in Him and to pass on His manner of sacrificial living to us and to all men throughout all ages, should have become the greatest factor in rending His Church asunder and keeping it a broken body.

Meaning of Sacrament

Thus through the familiar earthly symbols of bread and wine He fits His stature to our need, enters our hearts, and dwells in us. If we receive Him in faith, He will transform our stunted lives into the likeness of His own glorious stature, and will so fill us with His abundant life that, like branches attached to the living vine, we shall be nourished and sustained and enabled to bear much fruit. Let us therefore pray, as we approach this great service of healing and sustenance, that we may see it whole rather than in segments; that we may behold the cord and not the multiplicity of strands; the diamond and not the many facets; the rose and not the individual petals—for altar and table are alike His. He is "Lamb of God" as well as "Bread of Heaven." So whether or not we have been taught to emphasize the aspect of sacrifice, reconciliation, thanksgiving, love, hope, covenant, fellowship—let us never forget the redemptive significance and the unspeakable importance of the Sacrament in our growth in newness of life. Those of us who love the Church will always rejoice over John Wesley's devotion to this great Sacrament. William Palmer Ladd, of the Berkeley Divinity School, New Haven, Connecticut, says of the founder of Methodism:

> In the 18th century, the heyday of the Whig bishops, the easygoing parsons, and the infrequent Eucharists, a prophet arose in the person of John Wesley...he came to an understanding of sacramental theology by a study of the Fathers, of Jeremy Taylor and other Caroline divines, and of nonjuring churchmen like William Law.... He received communion weekly, and indeed as many as four times each week on the average throughout his entire ministry.... He urged the duty of constant communion. And his communion services attracted the common people beyond the capacity of the churches to hold them.[1]

[1] William Palmer Ladd, *Prayer Book Interleaves* (New York: Oxford University Press, 1942), pp. 18, 19. Used by permission.

We do well to follow Wesley to one of the sources of his power—the table of the Lord, and like him receive the royal Bread and "the royal Wine of heaven" for our cleansing, our quickening, and our sustaining. May our mood of approach be a fruitful blend of the awe of the Centurion: "Lord, I am not worthy that thou shouldest come under my roof"[1] and the ecstasy of Zacchaeus, for whom the entry of Jesus into his home necessitated fourfold amends for an unworthy past as well as the obligations of a future in which the shamefulness of extortion would be transformed into the magnificence of giving.[2]

Practicing the Presence

The fourth great channel through which we receive sustenance is the events of ordinary everyday living, in which we must strive to acquire Brother Lawrence's habit, practicing the Presence of God. There is nothing vague, or mystical, or impossible about this practice. If we are living in our Father's world, then it should be our chief business and joy to see Him everywhere in it. Jesus has made this practice of His Presence as easy and as natural for us as possible. He has stamped His image and superscription so indelibly on all the familiar objects round about us that, unless we are wilfully blind, we cannot avoid seeing Him in them several times a day. As we walk through a door, we hear Him saying, "I am the door." As we drive along a highway, "I am the way;" the wild flowers of the field whisper, "Consider the lilies." The meadows say, "If God so clothe the grass....;" the commonplace English sparrows chirp, "Ye are of more value than many sparrows." A flock of sheep pass by, and lo! He is both Lamb and Shepherd! And so on, bread, water, wine, candle, mountain, thornbrush, or tree, we find His imprint everywhere.

[1]Matt. 8:8.
[2]Luke 19:1-10.

But God comes to us not only in all the familiar objects of life; every experience of our lives can be made sacramental, an opening of our hearts for the Holy Spirit to fill us with His great all-embracing gift of love. No matter what the experience—sorrow, sickness, pain, anxiety, doubt, or despair—it can become a channel for His sustaining life, if with no bitterness or resentment, we simply turn to Him and say, "Father, glorify Thyself in me through this experience."

Unceasing Prayer

This constant practice of the Presence of God is in reality the mood of unceasing prayer. Many years ago I found the method very simply pointed out in a rather quaint story. A group of ministers, who met monthly, were discussing St. Paul's command, "Pray without ceasing." After a number of learned and not-too-satisfactory interpretations had been presented, the chairman commissioned one of the younger members to meditate upon the words and to write his reflections in the form of an essay, to be read at the next meeting. To their surprise, a servant, who happened to be listening, exclaimed, "What! wait a whole month to tell the meaning of one of the easiest texts in the Bible!" Half-amused and half-credulous, an old minister turned to her and said, "Tell us about it, Mary. You are always busy. Do you pray all the time?" "Oh, yes, sir!" she replied joyously. "The more I have to do, the more I pray. When I open my eyes in the morning, I ask God to open the eyes of my mind so that I may know Him better; while I am dressing, I ask Him to clothe me in His robe of righteousness; when I wash myself, I thank Him for the water of new birth; when I begin my work, I ask for strength sufficient for the task I am about to do; when I light the kitchen fire, I ask Him to kindle the flame of His love in my heart; when I start sweeping, I ask Him to cleanse my heart from all impurities; when I begin to prepare breakfast, I ask Him to feed me with heavenly food and with the milk of the Word; when I go out to play with the children, I ask Him to give me a child-like spirit. Why, sir, everything that I do makes me think of something to pray or to thank God for.''

The experience of this woman may well be ours if we will persevere in practicing God's Presence in everything we do. This is spiritual sustenance. This is feeding on Jesus. Every day we shall become more and more conscious of His nearness, more and more sure of God's fatherly hand upon our head, and more and more sensitive to the guidance of the Holy Spirit. In fact, our lives will become a glad fulfilment of His promise, ''Lo, I am with you alway, even unto the end of the world.''[1]

Fed to Feed

We have thought of some of the lessons contained in this key Sign, and have seen the essential part it plays in our growth in the newness of life. The more we reflect upon the Sign, the more truth it will reveal. But we must not leave it without noting the end and aim of its teaching: the fact that we are fed in order that we may feed others. Someone has said that each individual touches intimately about ten persons. These ten constitute our ''multitude'' for whom we must find bread. If we are faithful in feeding the ten assigned to us, then God will, as He sees fit, increase the number. No spiritual dearth in our lives must ever call forth that tragic confession of neglect and impotence: ''A friend of mine in his journey is come to me, and I have nothing to set before him.''[2] So day by day let us bring to Him our meager resources: ''Five loaves, dear Lord, and fishes only two!'' And He will take them in His creative hands and multiphy them as He breaks them for

[1]Matt. 28:20.
[2]Luke 11:6.

distribution. Then not only will our own sustenance be assured, but also shall we receive an ample supply (typified by the large baskets of fragments that remained) for all who come to us for food, and furthermore, we shall have a store of satisfying extras for any unexpected midnight need.

Chapter Five

Guidance

John 6:15-21
Walking on the Sea

When Jesus, therefore, perceived that they would come and take Him by force to make Him a king, He departed again into a mountain Himself alone. And when even was *now* come, His disciples went down unto the sea, and entered into a ship, and went over the sea toward Capernaum. And it was now dark, and Jesus was not come to them. And the sea arose by reason of a great wind that blew. So when they had rowed about five and twenty or thirty furlongs, they see Jesus walking on the sea, and drawing night unto the ship: and they were afraid. But He saith unto them, It is I; be not afraid. Then they willingly received Him into the ship: and immediately the ship was at the land whither they went.

The great central Sign, "The Feeding of the Five Thousand," on which we reflected in chapter four, had a setting suggestive of fellowship and bounty: a grassy slope at the base of a mountain. "Grass," says Matthew; "green grass," says Mark; "much green grass," says John. But now as we pass on to the fifth Sign, "The Walking on the Sea," the bright scene of springtime bounty vanishes. The peaceful green slope gives place to a stormy sea; the soft light of eventide is blacked-out in a long midnight of toil and terror; the Lord of Life and Light seems to have withdrawn His gracious Presence, and the separation from Him is marked by darkness. What necessary instruction can there be for our growth in newness of life in this Sign of mystery and awe?

Three Accounts Compared

As we read the three accounts in the Gospels[1] (for the majority of commentators are agreed that the three recordings relate one experience), we notice that Matthew and Mark stress the miraculous. Throughout the vivid scene they emphasize the doings of Jesus, the wonder-working Son of God. In their reports of the miracle, it is Jesus who sends the disciples away; who dismisses the multitude; who goes apart into the mountain to pray; who sees the disciples in distress, despite distance and black sea and blacker midnight; who comes to their aid, and yet is in the very act of passing by when they hail Him; who allays their fear, encourages Peter to step out on the angry water, and rescues him when faith succumbs to fear; who enters the boat and causes the storm to cease; and who receives their worship, which is called forth by the sore amazement caused by His deeds. But the author of the Fourth Gospel, more concerned with meaning than with miracle, purposely puts the disciples in the foreground; and

[1]John H. Kerr, *A Harmony of the Gospels* (Twelfth Edition Revised; New York: Fleming H. Revell Co., 1924), p. 89.

71

yet by this very natural presentation, he makes us all the more acutely conscious of Jesus—His prevenient Presence of light and power and love—God unseen, but ever intimately near, and as we read, we see the Savior as the great "backdrop of this spiritual drama, giving meaning to every move.

St. John impresses upon us the fact that the gracious Feeding of the Five Thousand meant little more to the crowd than food means to a "crop-filled bird." He shows us the satisfied and self-absorbed people hailing Jesus, not as the source and support of abundant life, but as a temporal leader whom they intend to compel to set up a material kingdom of plenty for their well-being. Because of their lack of understanding of Him and His mission, Jesus, whose sole concern is His Father's kingdom, withdraws from them to commune with His Father, and somehow the very statement of His withdrawal prepares our hearts for nightfall. The disciples leave Him and set out for home; darkness overtakes them; they battle with a rising sea in the stress of a mighty contrary wind—not the favorable wind of His Spirit. But in the hour of their direst need, they see Jesus and are afraid; they receive Him gladly into the boat; and lo! immediately they are in "port after stormy seas"!

Lessons of the Sign

This Sign is regarded as symbolic of the experience of the Church since the Ascension. Left alone, as it were for a time, without the visible presence of Jesus, it is tossed about on the sea of doubt and trouble and toil and fear; but when He "shall come again in his glorious majesty," He will still all storms, allay all doubts and fears, and immediately the Church will find herself, safe and victorious, in the haven of His love. And indeed this is a practical and essential lesson, for it comforts and nerves the "Holy Church throughout all the world" to keep on struggling against adverse winds and waves, strong in the truth that victory is sure. But other valuable lessons for individual Christians lie in this Sign, and we do well to consider what these lessons are.

Jesus Governs

First of all, this Sign teaches us that Jesus is Lord of our lives. We must acknowledge His governance before asking His guidance. His declaration of His sovereignty is crystal clear: "Ye call me Master and Lord; and ye say well; for so I am."[1] Feeding anticipates following. The new strength received from Him is not our own to be used for selfish purposes—but puts us under obligation to follow wherever He leads. It is to be consecrated to the furtherance of His kingdom through the doing of His will. God stoops to feed us, but He cannot stoop to fall in with *our* plans. If, therefore, in the rash hardihood of our strong powers, we turn aside from His way and venture forth on our own, we find ourselves in darkness. St. John uses the words "darkness" and "night" as symbolic of opposition to, or separation from, Jesus.

In Norse mythology there is a grim story of how two wolves pursued the sun and moon, finally overtook and swallowed them, and the light was blotted out in the terrible darkness known as the Twilight of the Gods. But St. John says, "The light shines in the darkness, and the darkness has not overcome it."[2] He knows that light has nothing to fear from the darkness, for the very nature of light makes it victorious; and so he uses a Greek verb with a double significance to assure us that darkness can neither "grasp with the mind" and so "comprehend" light,[3] nor "grasp with the hand" and so "overcome" or "destroy" light.[4]

The light shines, an eternal present, offering life and direction to all who walk in it. "Lord, lead, and I follow" must be the glad commitment of all who feed on Him.

[1]John 13:13. KJV.   [3]John 1:5. KJV says "The darkness *comprehendeth* it not."
[2]John 1:5. RSV.   [4]Cf. Sir Edwin Hoskyns, *The Fourth Gospel, op cit.,* pp. 5, 143.

Jesus Guides

But side by side with the truth that Jesus governs, stands the twin truth that Jesus guides. "Direct us, O Lord, in all our doings, with thy most gracious favor..." runs the petition in the collect for God's continued help.[1] The *all* is important, for Jesus is concerned with the whole of life. No area in our lives may be shut off from His Presence. This Sign teaches us that He manifests His glory as perfectly on stormy waters as in peaceful pastures. Lord of our gladness, he is Lord also of our gloom. This is a truth that we learned when we were children from the beautiful hymn by Cecil F. Alexander.

> And He feeleth for our sadness,
> And He shareth in our gladness.[2]

He has a plan of life for each one of us, and every move made under His guidance is definitely related to His whole well-ordered plan. We must know that no matter how baffling the experience, the hand of the Father is always over His child. All He requires is that we receive Him "into the boat" of our sorrow, doubt, lack, sickness, bereavement, fear—or whatever the circumstance happens to be—and immediately He will manifest His glory by sanctifying the experience to us as a means of spiritual growth.

When I was confirmed, I was given a tiny book called *Spiritual Letters of St. Francis de Sales*. It looked dry and uninteresting, but my affection for the giver and my faith in his wise guidance constrained me to read it. The first letter was to a novice who was worried about her feelings; the second was to a priest who was about to be consecrated bishop. Both letters seemed boring and utterly removed from the experience of a girl living in the twentieth century. But I went on to the third which was addressed to "Madame Rose Bourgeois."

[1] The Book of Common Prayer.
[2] Lines from the Christmas hymn "Once in Royal David's City".

I remember thinking what an odd combination of names—
"Rose" so suggestive of beauty; "Bourgeois" so suggestive
of the commonplace. Then I began the letter, and I recall
the opening words as though I read them yesterday. "Your
father has told me how much you are suffering.... The Lord
be praised!" Young as I was, the unexpectedness of the
words startled me out of my superficial mood. I had happened
upon what was to me a brand new type of condolence. A
Bishop hears of someone in intense pain, and instead of
writing, "I am so sorry for you," or "You have my deepest
sympathy," or "My heart aches for you,"—or any of the
similar normal responses that we rather expect, and usually
receive, when we are ill—sends the sufferer only ringing
words of joy! "The Lord be praised!" Here was my initiation,
as it were, into that triumphant, alleluia-all-the-way-home
expression of joyous faith which I have since found to be the
hallmark of all valiant saints—Stephen, Paul, Polycarp—just
to start a list of that multitude which no man can number, the
named and the unnamed, every century adding its quota,
ancient and modern ages linked together in an almost incre-
dible audacity of rejoicing when brought face to face with
the dark mystery of pain—a mood which each heroic heart
caught and passed on from One "who for the joy that was
set before Him endured the cross, despising the shame."[1] It is
this unshaken trust in the overruling providence of God that
this Sign would teach us. Jesus knows and cares and comes.

Glad Trust in Jesus

To acknowledge the authority of Jesus to govern, to trust
His wisdom to guide, to receive Him and thus welcome all
the doings and happenings of our lives as opportunities for
praising and blessing His holy Name—these are lessons
that must be mastered if we are to grow in the newness of life.
Throughout the ages spiritual guides have known that in each

[1]Heb. 12:2.

75

individual life green pastures do give way to stormy seas, and the brightness of His Presence does become blacked-out in the "Dark Night of the Soul," but they also know that he who is a quickening flame within and a presence round about, is Lord trimphant of storm and of darkness, making them fulfil and obey His word. These are the truths that shine forth in the Bible, in the lives of the saints, and in our greatest hymns. If these teachings seem to us foolishness, it is that we have not yet mastered their language. The greatness of surrender that we find in them is disturbing to our self-cherishing outlook. It is we who are at fault, not they. That consecrated clergyman, scholar, and hymn writer, Dr. Horatius Bonar of Scotland, wrote a hymn that most certainly must have grown out of the author's years of devoted vigil with Jesus in Gethsemane, for in it we seem to hear the Savior's words as He practiced in completeness what He had earlier taught His disciples about the priority of God: "Not as I will, but as thou wilt."

> Thy way, not mine, O Lord,
>   However dark it be:
> Lead me by Thine own hand;
>   Choose out the path for me.
> Smooth let it be or rough,
>   It still *will* be the best;
> Winding or straight it leads
>   Right onward to Thy rest.
>
> Choose Thou my friends for me,
>   My sickness or my health;
> Choose Thou my cares for me,
>   My poverty or wealth.
> Not mine, not mine the choice
>   In things both great or small
> Be *Thou* my Guide, my Strength,
>   My Wisdom, and my All.

These lines sum up our longing for the governance and guidance of God. When we make these words our own prayer, we seem to touch the reality with which the author has grappled. Such prayer is a bringing forth from the treasury of our hearts a glad sacrifice of praise and faith kindled by love. St. Augustine saw this spirit of triumphant surrender in Job. He tells us that after everything had been taken away from Job "at one swoop,...alone there remained Job"! He goes on to observe, "Hear what he had. Hear what he brought forth: 'The Lord hath given, the Lord hath taken away; as hath pleased the Lord, so hath he done: be the name of the Lord blessed.' O riches interior!"[1]

Need of Guidance

Do not these rapturous words of power and conviction, uttered in an experience of desolation—such as thousands of innocent people in England, Europe, and Asia have known and still know—make our hearts burn within us to bring forth our sacrifice of faith and praise and love? Do we not long more than anything else to make the rule and direction of God a reality in our lives?

Step by step, through the Signs of the Fourth Gospel, St. John shows us how our storehouse of interior riches may be enlarged and filled. Day by day we are enriched, taught to trust; we are restored, sustained—but without guidance all health and energy are vain. Jesus must be pilot of our "boat" as well as captain. Too often our lives are indicative of aimless, misdirected, futile energy—perhaps "hurry" is the truer term! We are like the lecturer who, on finding himself almost late for an appointment, jumped into a taxi and told the driver, "Drive fast!" "After a considerable period of skidding around corners and speeding down narrow streets, he shouted..., 'Aren't we almost there?' 'I haven't

---

[1] St. Augustine, Homily on Psalm 76:11.

the faintest idea, sir,' came back the prompt reply. 'You never told me where you wanted to go. All you said to me was drive fast, and I've been a-doing it.' "[1]

In the Lord's Prayer, Jesus revealed His knowledge of this devastating aimlessness by listing food, forgiveness, and guidance as our essential needs. And in the tenderest chapters of St. John's Gospel—13 through 17—called by Sir Edwin Hoskyns the "Ideal Eucharist"—Jesus promised to pray the Father to send the Holy Spirit who will lead us into all truth. What a glorious trinity of concern for our welfare— as Bishop Ryle points out—"The Son praying, the Father giving, the Spirit comforting."

"Grant that this day we fall into no sin, neither run into any kind of danger; but that all our doings may be ordered by Thy governance...."[2] "By Thy great mercy defend us from all perils and dangers of this night."[3]

The Holy Spirit Transforms

It is, therefore, imperative that all who would walk in newness of life keep on asking, seeking, and knocking, until God's direction and rule are evident in all departments of our lives—in home, in office, in school, in shop, in hospital, in social centers—wherever our lifework lies. And not only in working hours but also in periods of relaxation and recreation—in fact, in the four main spheres of activity in which we live: home, church, place of work, and place of amusement.

Evelyn Underhill suggests that the main causes of disharmony in our lives are "inclinations to selfish choices, inordinate enjoyments, claimful affection, self-centered worry, instinctive avoidance of sacrifice and pain...."[4] Let us think

[1]Carl Hopkins Elmore, *Quit You Like Men* (New York: Charles Scribner's Sons, 1944), p. 4.

[2]Collect from Morning Prayer, Book of Common Prayer.

[3]Collect from Evening Prayer and Compline.

[4]Evelyn Underhill, *The House of the Soul* (New York: E. P. Dutton & Co., Inc., 1930), p. 22.

honestly about each of these causes. Do any of them show up in our dealings with ourselves or with others? The sevenfold gift of the Holy Spirit provides the special grace required for the overcoming of each specific weakness or fault of character, for grace is the "energy of the Holy Spirit working in us," transforming, illuminating, leading. What a blossoming begins in the gardnes of our hearts as soon as we permit Him to brood on the barren, uncultivated soil: "love, joy, peace, longsuffering, gentleness, goodness, faith, meekness, temperance."[2] What a transfiguration would take place—first in ourselves, and then in home, church, community, nation, world—if every member of the Christian Church could possess and practice these gifts that may be obtained only through the indwelling of the Holy Spirit: no malicious gossip, no unkind words, no snap judgments, no prejudices, no greed, no self-seeking—nothing but divine Love at work within each of us, expressing Himself through us with the Godlike impartiality of air and sun and rain—healing all wounds, binding up broken hearts, freeing captives from the chains of sin or circumstance, showing forth the glory of God in a larger understanding and a deeper sympathy—and binding us in God's "living tether" into a great compassionate "Fellowship of the Concerned" as Elton Trueblood has termed the Church.

Are we sincere enough to enlist in His work of new creation? Are we sturdy enough day after day to accept the obligations of a life of prayer and praise? Do we really long to "walk and not be weary" as we press gladly on toward the perfection to which Jesus so emphatically and so joyously calls us? If so, then let us consider the nature and power and use of silence in our spiritual development, the silence that is still silence in our spiritual development, the silence that is stillness before God—listening to Him and receiving from Him; for the practice of silence must now become a part of the discipline of our life of devotion.

[1]Gal. 5:22, 23.

79

Nature of Silence

In order to receive guidance, we must learn to be still and wait upon God. Yet it is amazing how small a part silence plays in the lives of average Christians, even of those who have taken upon themselves the obligations of church membership. This neglect is due largely to a misunderstanding of the true nature of silence. Many of us think of silence as a negative quality, having occult associations that class it with fads or sensational "-isms"—an artificial attitude, or pose, suggestive of show rather than of sense. We are inclined to sympathize with the husband who said to his wife on her return from a week-end retreat: "You mean you paid good money just to sit still?" But there is nothing barren, showy or unreal about silence as revealed in the Bible and in the lives of spiritual leaders.

Silence: An Attribute of God

And it is not surprising that in earlier ages God was spoken of as "The Silence," for beginning with the idyllic prelude of Genesis, in which we hear the voice of God at eventide in the cool stillness of the Garden of Eden, the Old Testament reveals silence as an attribute of God Himself—the nature of His creative energy.

"The Lord is in His holy temple: let all the earth keep silence before Him."[1] "Hold thy peace at the presence of the Lord God."[2] "Be silent, O all flesh, before the Lord."[3]

In this connection Dr. William Badè gives a most helpful and illuminating translation of Isaiah 18:4—"Thus the Lord said to me, 'I will be still, and will look on in my place, like the flickering ether of sunlight, like dew-clouds in the heat

[1] Hab. 2:20.
[2] Zeph. 1:7.
[3] Zech. 2:13.

of harvest."[1] What a picture of the silent productive activity and the sovereignty of God, sitting still and looking down upon His universe, the work of His hands, and infiltrating Himself through every part of it, as the sunshine interpenetrates the air on a rare June day! Here is a conception of God as Silence paralleling St. John's conception of Him as Light. Silence, by its very nature victorious, has nothing to fear from noise. Despite all the tumult that our wayward wills continue to make in His world, God can be still and look on in His place, knowing that eventually "in returning and rest we shall be saved, in quietness and confidence shall be our strength."[2] He would indeed spare us all the anguish that our refusal to accept His will brings upon us; but until that glad day of our returning, He waits—the creative silence of His everlasting love filled to overflowing with the fruits of His Spirit, which He is eager and ready to rain upon us in blessings, even as the dew was supposed to fall from the high clouds at harvest time.

> He shall come down like showers
> Upon the fruitful earth,
> Love, joy, and hope, like flowers,
> Spring in His path to birth:
> Before Him, on the mountains,
> Shall peace, the herald, go,
> And righteousness, in fountains,
> From hill to valley flow.[3]

What a certainty of the victory of silence over noise! And how we long to dedicate ourselves to the hastening in of that "time that shall surely be"!

[1]William Frederic Badè, *The Old Testament in the Light of Today* (Sixth Impression, 1922; New York: Houghton Mifflin Company, 1915), p. 183.
[2]Prayer "For Quiet Confidence," *The Book of Common Prayer.*
[3]James Montgomery.

Silence: An Attribute of Jesus

The Bible, however, shows silence to be not only a property of God the Father, but also an attribute of God the Son; for in the foreshadowing of the ineffable mystery of Emmanuel—("How wonderful that God should be with man!")—we are conscious of silence: "He shall not cry, nor lift up, nor cause His voice to be heard in the street."[1] No sensational, noisy heralding; no soap-box type of oratory, but, "He was oppressed, and He was afflicted, yet He opened not His mouth."[2] And when in humble love we follow Emmanuel to Pilate's judgment seat, we still read: "And He gave him no answer, not even to a single charge; that the governor wondered greatly."[3] Here we find the same quiet certitude characteristic of Him who said, "I will be still and look on in my place." And we find it again in that culminating picture that must not be omitted: "In the midst of the throne...stood a Lamb as though it had been slain."[4] as we read that fifth chapter of Revelation—above the tumult of acclamation, above the joyful strains of the new song bursting forth from the four living creatures, the four and twenty elders, and the attendant angels—the only voice that the soul hears is the silent voice of the Lamb, now standing creatively alert in the midst of the throne prepared for Him "from the foundation of the world," and crying out in the endless, voiceless intercession that mankind may be saved. Truly the Son "of one substance with the Father by whom all things were made![5]"

Silence Required of Man

But the Old Testament has a further revelation of silence. It sets it forth as a quality required of man, if he would hear God's commands or see any revelation of God's glory. "Stand

[1]Isa. 42:2. KJV.   [4]Rev. 5:6. RSV.
[2]Isa. 53:7. KJV.   [5]Nicene Creed.
[3]Matt. 27:14. RSV.

still and see the salvation of the Lord, which He will shew you today,"[1] says Moses, to the terrified Israelites who are being pursued by Pharaoh's hosts. "Stand still, and I will hear what the Lord will command concerning you,"[2] he admonishes them during their desert pilgrimage, as he organizes their civil and religious life. "Stand still first," says Samuel to Saul before anointing him, "that I may cause you to hear the word of God."[3] "O Job, stand still, and consider the wondrous works of God,"[4] advises Elihu, just as God is about to speak, for the enlightenment of Job, the words of golden splendor that we find recorded in the eighth scene of that great drama. "Be still and know that I am God,"[5] says the psalmist in words so stamped with authority of faith that they have supported throughout succeeding ages those who stagger under the stress of battle or the strain of daily living, words which inspired Luther to write his battle cry of faith: "A Mighty Fortress Is Our God." Thus lawgiver, prophet, poet, and psalmist show us God eternally creative, yet eternally at rest, and make us aware of the "unutterable harmonious silence which guards inviolate the courts of Heaven's high Majesty,"[6] and they instruct us as we draw near to put on the reuired and beautiful garment of stillness and serenity, if we would gain audience.

Children Receptive

Children are receptive to silence, if wisely guided in the practice of it, and we older ones are responsible for transmitting its power to the young. My first interest in silence grew out of great creative experience in my childhood, when the wings of the Most High were overshadowing me, though I knew it not. It happened on the Good Friday after my

---

[1]Exod. 14:13.
[2]Num. 9:8.
[3]I Sam. 9:27. (Amplified).
[4]Job 37:14.

[5]Ps. 46:10.
[6]Bede Frost. *The Return to God* (London: Church Literature Association, 1934), p. 111.

twelfth birthday. Year after year I had heard of the three-hour service which followed the regular eleven o'clock Morning Prayer. There was a break before twelve, so that children and older people who did not want to stay might leave. I was curious to find out what people did in church for three hours, after having already been there for one hour. "They contemplate the cross," my father said—mystifying words which whetted my curiousity still more, for it seemed to me, then, that one could see all there was to be seen of the cross in a much shorter period of time than that. He said that I might stay on for the second service, after I was twelve. I have never forgotten how grown up I felt as other children and adults left, and I remained with the quiet group who yearly embraced the discipline of a four-hour service for love of Jesus. On our knees we began to sing Faber's realistic hymn: "O Come and Mourn With Me a While." As we sang the first two stanzas, my imagination made a vivid picture of the supreme agony of Jesus. I seemed to see Him actually hanging there, so patiently, before the jeering crowds. My eyes filled with tears, the first I had ever shed for Him who loved me and gave Himself for me—and my mother, noticing my struggle with hymnbook and handkerchief, put a steadying arm around me. But we passed on to the third stanza, and the mysterious contradiction which it expressed occupied my mind rather than my heart, and dried my tears:

> Seven times He spake, seven words of love;
> And all three hours His silence cried
> For mercy on the souls of men:
> Jesus, our Lord, is crucified.

The great paradox expressed in the words, "His silence cried," occupied my mind for the rest of the service. Late that afternoon it was still disturbing me. "How can silence cry?" I asked my father. "If it cries, it isn't silence." "The voice of silence is a voiceless voice," he replied, in true St.

Augustine vein. "Keep on thinking about it. Try to listen to it; and you will hear it." A crying silence! a voiceless voice! How past finding out is the language of eternal verities! How veiled in mist is the path toward the eternal Silence which the seeking soul must travel! Yet, in just such natural and quiet ways, do the Everlasting Doors lift up their heads in the heart of a child!

A Creative Activity

Thus we see that silence, which is so important in our growth in newness of life, is no negative barren condition, but the intense activity of creative love, the breath of God at work in the garden of the soul. The prophet Zephaniah gives us a picture of the cherishing tenderness of the Almighty: "The Lord thy God in the midst of thee is mighty; He will save, He will rejoice over thee with joy; He will rest in His love, He will joy over thee with singing."[1] Here is God intent on bringing forth His own abundant life into the heart of each one of His children who is willing to be passive and receptive beneath His brooding love. It seems to me that St. John of the Cross sums up all that can be said about the nature of silence in these significant words: "The Father uttered one word: that Word is His Son, and He utters Him forever in an eternal silence, and in silence must the soul hear. That which we most require for our spiritual growth is the silence of the desire and of the tongue before God who is so high: the language He most listens to is that of silent love."

Cultivation of Silence

How can we cultivate this creative silence—of stilled tongue and stilled desire—the voiceless language of love to which the Father delights to listen and which enables us to hear more perfectly His uttered Word? If we are in earnest, we

[1]Zeph. 3:17. KJV.

shall begin at once, and be willing to go slowly, like children learning a new language, for mastery of the first simple exercises will ensure a more effective use of silence later on.

Exterior Silence

Let us therefore begin with the rudimentary steps—the new alphabet as it were—the practice of exterior silence. This type of silence is an outward indication of an inner self-restraint, and is of inestimable value. First, in our relation to things: when we were young, were we not often told that "to close a door quietly is the hallmark of a lady?" It should also be hallmark of a Christian! Now we must make a point of closing doors quietly, of handling things gently—the silver, the dishes, the kitchen utensils—all the many things in our homes that need not be used noisily if we exert a little self-discipline. One quiet meal a week is another excellent practice, teaching us to observe and anticipate the needs of others, and training us to pass and put down things noiselessly.

Next, in our relation to people: this means speaking quietly, laughing quietly, moving among them quietly. Someone has suggested that God puts us to live in buildings that have no soundproof walls, so that we may practice being quiet! And some of us remember Dr. Fosdick's story of the woman who prayed for patience and, when God sent her an impossible cook, did not see that the cook was the answer to her prayer.

Then in our relation to ourselves: this means the discipline of learning to be still! Some of us are actually afraid of being silent. We are like the very talkative woman who was prevailed upon to go to her first week-end retreat. After supper, when the conductor announced that silence would be observed until after breakfast on Monday morning, she turned to her friend and blurted out in mingled indignation and horror: "You mean I'm not to say a single word until Monday morning! I'm going home!" But the majority of us are more emotionally stable than she was. We must learn to control our bodies by making ourselves sit still without fidgeting. A conductor at a retreat once gave this helpful and vivid suggestion: "When you are trying to keep still as you sit or kneel, and feel a strong inclination to move, think of yourself as nailed to a cross." The important thing behind all this practice is that we must be severe with ourselves. We must make ourselves do what we set out to do— even if at first we keep very brief periods of stillness. It is largely a matter of will power.

Interior Silence

Now let us consider the far harder discipline of interior silence. For even after we have learned to be outwardly still, we may be inwardly restless. The faculties of the mind are more difficult to control than the impulses of the body, and the "squirrel-in-a-cage" type of mind is more unruly than an unbroken colt. But eternal vigilance will bring us victory. Let us sit quietly and try to still the senses—hearing and seeing in particular. Close our eyes, and in the restful darkness try to shout out sounds. Then begin to still our minds. Let us be relaxed, for anxiety creates tension and defeats our aim. It will take years of faithful practice to gain complete control of the complex mind, with its faculties of intellect, understanding, memory, imagination, and will, and put them to work in a new way. A good first step is to center our thoughts on Jesus. Imagine ourselves in the position of Mary Magdalene beside the empty tomb on the first Easter morning, kneeling at the feet of the risen Savior and saying, as she looks up in glad adoration, the one word, "Master!"[1] Or see ourselves like Thomas, gazing in humility and love at the wounds of the risen Lord, and uttering the triumphant words of joyous faith, "My Lord and my God!"[2] Keep our attention

[1] John 20:16.
[2] John 20:28.

87

fixed on Jesus; and with patient determination bring back our thoughts to Him every time they seem to wander. There must be no tenseness, no anxiety, no distress, if at the start we fail to concentrate—just a quiet persistent effort to turn our thoughts to our Lord. These periods of concentration should be very brief at first, and then be lengthened gradually as our power of concentration grows. Exterior silence may be practiced at any time, but interior silence should have set periods. We can use it before and after our morning and evening prayer; before and after our daily Bible reading. In fact, we must train ourselves at the close of every period of devotion to wait in silence for His benediction: "Peace I leave with you, My peace I give unto you."[1]

In Corporate Worship

But silence makes also a valuable contribution to corporate worship. We should plan to be in church at least ten minutes before the service begins. During that time we should rest in silence before God, thinking of ourselves as empty spiritually, waiting to be filled. It must be an expectant waiting, a longing to be filled with His fulness. Meister Eckhart has some wise words in this connection: "The soul that grows while it is being filled will never be full." Let us think of our "interior castle" as sensitive to the action of the Holy Spirit—not set and hard, but expanding, even as the psalmist imagined the very doors of the Temple to be lifting themselves up at the approach of the King of glory: "Lift up your heads, O ye gates; even lift them up, ye everlasting doors; and the King of glory shall come in."[2] Or we may visualize St. Augustine's prayer: "Narrow is the mansion of my soul, enlarge Thou it, that Thou mayest enter in. It is ruinous; repair Thou it."

Pauses in the service should be used as listening times— "Speak, Lord; for thy servant heareth."[3] We can form the

[1]John 14:27.
[2]Ps. 24:9.
[3]I Sam. 3:9.

88

habit of staying our mind on some attribute of God: His majesty, His silence, His patience, His compassion. When prayers are being offered during the service, there is great value in a corporate lifting up of our petitions to God in silent love and then relinquishing them to His will, knowing that all is well. Our first steps in the practice of silence will be slow, but if we persevere, the whole temper of our lives will be changed.

Quiet Days and Retreats

But perhaps the most valuable aids in the practice of creative silence are quiet days and retreats. They have become an established and systematic part of the spiritual life in England, and have been growing in number and in popularity in this country. Many religious houses invite individuals and groups to have quiet days or retreats at regular intervals throughout the year, so that everyone who is in earnest has an opportunity to find out at firsthand what an ordered practice of silence can do for the growing soul. The aim of quiet days and retreats is perhaps most perfectly expressed in the words of a second-century saint: "Ask for larger wisdom than thou hast." We enter a retreat to ask guidance from God, so that His rule in our hearts may be more complete. We come to listen in order that we may know what His plan is for us, as lay workers in His Church, and how He wants us to carry out that plan. One of the great devotional classics is *The Spiritual Exercises* of Ignatius Loyola (late fifteenth century), written for use in retreats. Although the excercises are complicated, they contain a wealth of material on the art of meditation and the value of silence. They stress the primary value of silence: to listen to God; to learn His plan for us; to receive directions for carrying out that plan; and they emphasize our obligation to follow those directions when we come out of the silence.

Plan for Quiet Day

Perhaps a brief suggestion of how to plan a quiet day in a retreat house or in a church, without a conductor, may give some idea of the pattern of an ordered silence. We must decide upon a theme. An excellent first one is given by St. Ignatius—"Our Creation." Let us use as a key thought: "We bless thee for our creation," and ask the Holy Spirit to help us to know the purpose for which we were created, to give us grace to keep it constantly before our minds, and to help us to live so that we may fulfil it by praising, reverencing, and serving God. Plan three meditations of about twenty minutes each on this theme: the first from 10:00 to 10:20 a.m.; the second from 12:00 noon to 12:20 p.m.; and the third from 2:30 to 2:50 p.m. In the first meditation, take the thought: "O God, Thou hast created me." Think of the time when we existed in the heart and mind of God, but had not yet been brought into being on this earth. Then think of the time when God made and fashioned us, using our parents as the human instruments to give us physical being; think of the hopes and expectations our parents had for us when we were born; but remember that God created us, and that in Him "we live and move and have our being."[1]

The second meditation might be on the theme: "Why did God create me?" Let us recall that He created us so that we might share in His abundant life and love. Love was the sole reason for our creation. Let us go on to consider that He created us to fill a particular place and to do a particular work, making us in His own image and giving us a relationship dearer and higher than that of the angels—the relationship of sons and daughters. And all He asks in return for all this wondrous love is that we love Him and fulfil His plan for us—never forgetting that "for His pleasure we were and are created."

[1] Acts 17:28.

The third meditation might be on: "How can I love and serve God?" Let us think upon the "one thing needful"—"Thou shalt worship the Lord thy God, and Him only shalt thou serve."[1] Then let us try to realize that our happiness lies in this worship and love of God. "Great peace have they which love Thy law."[2] And finally let us ponder the amazing truth that love cannot compel. God does not force us to love or serve Him. He gives us the right to choose. The decision lies with us: will we frustrate or fulfil His plan for us?

The time in between these set periods of meditation should be spent in silence—in sitting, kneeling, walking—not straining to think about God, but conscious of His Presence within and about us. We may use some book, either brought for the purpose or borrowed from a book table on which helpful literature is usually placed. It is wise to choose one book that seems to bear on the subject and stick to that. But before coming out of the quiet day, we must form a practical resolution which must be carried out faithfully until the next day; using St. Paul's question, "Lord, what wilt Thou have me to do?"[3] will help us in forming this resolution. But whatever the decision—it may be to correct some particular defect of character—we should write it down, renew it every morning, and check on it every evening. The real value of quiet days—or retreats, which are only extended quiet days—lies in *making a definite resolution,* and faithfully carrying it out in the days that follow—until our ordered lives confess the beauty of His peace.

Healing Power of Silence

But there is another aspect of silence that must be mentioned—the healing, curative power it has on our souls and bodies. In *Creative Prayer,* Mrs. E. Herman tells of a woman

[1]Matt. 4:10. KJV.
[2]Ps. 119:165. KJV.
[3]Acts 9:6. KJV.

who said, "My mother taught me that arnica was good for bruised flesh, and silence was good for a bruised soul." Silence does have the restorative power that Shakespeare saw sleep to possess. It does indeed "knit up the ravell'd sleeve of care"; it is the "balm of hurt minds" and "sore labour's bath"; but over and above all this remedial action, silence possesses the creativeness of Spirit—the Holy Spirit brooding on our hearts—in the inspired words of Gerard Manley Hopkins—"with warm breast, and with, ah, bright wings."[1]

In conclusion, is not the supreme conception of silence—its nature, its power, its sustenance—contained in the following revelation of the infinite loving-kindness of our God? "How often would I have gathered thy children together, even as a hen gathereth her chickens under her wings...!"[2] God grant that it may never be said of us "and ye would not!"

[1]Gerard Manley Hopkins, "God's Grandeur," *The Oxford Book of English Mystical Verse* (New York: Oxford University Press, 1916), p. 355.
[2]Matt. 23:37.

Chapter Six

Illumination

John 9:1-7

The Healing of the Man Born Blind

And as Jesus passed by, He saw a man which was blind
from *his* birth. And His disciples asked Him, saying,
Master, who did sin, this man, or his parents, that he
was born blind? Jesus answered, Neither hath this man
sinned, nor his parents: but that the works of God
should be made manifest in him. I must work the
works of Him that sent me, while it is day: the night
cometh, when no man can work. As long as I am in
the world, I am the light of the world. When He had
thus spoken, He spat on the ground, and made clay of
the spittle, and He anointed the eyes of the blind man
with the clay, and said unto him, Go, wash in the pool
of Siloam, (which is by interpretation, Sent.) He went
his way therefore, and washed, and came seeing.

An imperative need of the growing soul is illumination: "Send out thy light and thy truth: let them lead me."[1] This enlightenment, however, is not a restoration of sight, but a free and glorious gift of new vision, a gift of grace. This sixth Sign, "The Healing of the Man Born Blind," comes upon us like the roseburst of sunrise. It recalls that glorious morning at the Brook Jabbok, when, after Jacob's black night of wrestling "as he passed over Penuel, the sun rose upon him."[2] The Bible at times takes on the qualities of a stupendous epic, extolling the triumph of the Sun of Righteousness—from the prologue: "Let there be light,"[3] in Genesis, to the epilogue, "There shall be no night there,"[4] in Revelation. In the great hymn of creation with which the Bible begins, the triumph of light is anticipated in the six-times-repeated lyrical phrase, "and the evening and the morning." When I was very young, and my father was teaching me to read that great poem, I was surprised at what seemed to be the wrong order, and wanted to know why it wasn't written "correctly," "the morning and the evening." "We see life as night following morning," explained my father; "but God sees it as it really is—day following night, light following darkness, life following death." Dr. Alfred Plummer says that "the majesty of the first verse of St. John's Gospel surpasses all. The Son of Thunder opens with a peal."[5] It is fitting that this peal should be reminiscent of the hymn of creation; for the author's theme is the victory of the light of truth over the darkness of error. The outstanding mission of the Messiah was to be "a light to lighten the Gentiles" and to give "sight to the blind." Thus in chapters eight and nine, which relate to the sixth Sign, St. John shows how Jesus manifested, first by word and then by deed, that He is the Light of the World.

[1]Ps. 43:3.
[2]Gen. 32:31.
[3]Gen. 1:3.
[4]Rev. 22:5.
[5]The Cambridge Bible for Schools and Colleges.

Setting of Sign

Let us consider the setting of this sixth Sign. The brethren of our Lord had urged him to go up to Jerusalem—if He were really the Messiah—and show forth His miraculous works there at the Feast of the Tabernacles. This feast, which lasted eight days, is one of the three great festivals of the Jewish year. Their Passover corresponds to our Easter; their Pentecost, to our Whitsuntide; and their Tabernacles, to our Michaelmas. It was a happy autumn feast, held at the close of the harvest—a sort of "Harvest Home"—when the year's store of fruit and grain had been gathered in. Throughout the feast the thankful people, in holiday mood, lived in booths or tents, in remembrance of the temporary shelters which had been used during the years in the wilderness![1] Indeed, so gay was the feast that it had given rise to the proverb: "The man who has not seen these festivities does not know what a jublilee is." The religious activities, however, were marked by solemn ritual, centering around the symbols of water and light. Every day for seven days water was drawn in a golden vessel from the historic pool of Siloam and poured on the great altar, while the people sang the twelfth chapter of Isaiah, accompanied by trumpet blasts and hallelujahs. This was in commemoration of the goodness of God, who had made water gush from the rock in the wilderness. Beginning on the first night, the twin ceremony of light was also enacted. The great golden-branched candlesticks in the Court of the Women were lighted, and we are told that "they illumined the whole city." These lights were symbolic of the Pillar of Fire that for many years had led the Children of Israel through the pathless wilderness—a flame by night, a cloud by day.

---

[1] Lev. 23:39-42.

Water and Light

Jesus does not comply with the request to go up and display His powers at the Feast. At His temptation He had definitely renounced the spectacular, which makes so strong an appeal to worldly minds. His chosen way was "not to strive, nor cry," "nor lift up His voice in the street." The Son of God has no need to court public favor. But about the middle of the feast He does go up alone to teach in the temple courts, and His great controversy with the Jews begins. Day after day He proclaims Himself as the fulfilment of Hebrew prophecy, foretells His Passion, Death, and Resurrection, and rebukes the spiritual blindness that cannot see His Divine origin and mission because of His humble birth and because He has not been taught in their rabbinical schools. Then, on the eighth day of the feast when no water was drawn, He offers Himself to them as the fount of living water, in words so clear, so authoritative, and so wondrous in meaning, that they deserve to be written in letters of gold: "If any one thirst, let him come to me and drink. He who believes on me, as the scripture has said, out of his heart shall flow rivers of living water."[1] But this divine appeal falls on deaf ears, and His divine Presence is invisible to blind eyes. A few believe, many are puzzled, and the religious leaders oppose Him bitterly and plan His death. Despite the heartbreak caused by their opposition, He keeps on. Either on the last night of the feast, when the lights are not lighted, or early on the last morning, as He watched the rising sun flooding the temple walls, He proclaims Himself as the reality behind both candle and sun: "I am the light of the world: He who follows me will not walk in darkness, but will have the light of life."[2]

[1] John 7:37, 38. RSV.
[2] John 8:12.

It is in vain. They want Him neither as Enlightener nor as Liberator. And when He finally identifies Himself with God by taking His own name the sacred "I AM,"[1] they break into a frenzy, accuse Him of blasphemy, and pick up stones to cast at Him. But with that quiet power the bears silent witness to the truth of His words, He passes through their midst; and as He passes with that divine compassion that has ever been a quality of "the God of Abraham, the God of Isaac, and the God of Jacob," He demonstrates in deed what He has proclaimed in words.

Light of the World

A man, blind from birth, but possessing, as is revealed later, the eye of faith undimmed, arouses the interest of the disciples. The fact that the man is there at that very moment, presenting a striking contrast to those who have physical sight, but are spiritually stone-blind, savors more of the unfolding of God's plan than of mere coincidence. The disciples, obviously stirred by the tense struggle that had just reached a climax, pause before Him, and put to Jesus the age-old question, the "why" of suffering. Is affliction—this man's terrible blindness from birth, for example—the result of personal sin or the sin of one's parents? Surely a baby born blind did not sin before birth. Are parents' sins indeed visited upon children? What of Ezekiel's declaration of individual responsibility: "The son shall not bear the iniquity of the father, neither shall the father bear the iniquity of the son?"[2]

But Jesus never encourages fruitless argument or vain prying into people's lives. He gives a constructive approach to suffering. Satan can bind men in affliction, as he bound Job, but God can overrule such suffering and show forth His glory in it. Even so, this sufferer is about to have the works

[1]John 8:58.
[2]Ezek. 18:20.

98

of God made manifest in his blindness. How we wish we might see into the heart of the man as he hears so unusual a discussion of his condition! Must he not feel a stirring of hope as the most authoritative, the most compassionate, the most honest voice he has ever heard associates the glory of God with his lifelong affliction? Why doesn't he cry out for healing, as other blind men had done when Jesus was close at hand? Has the fact that blindness from birth had never been cured given a finality to his despair and made a request for healing seem futile? We can almost see him straining his ears in the darkness, fearful lest he should lose a word of the mysterious conversation. Then he catches those words of still stranger import, for he knows nothing of the nature and wonder of light: "I am the light of the world." A pause, and then the unforgettable touch of the Master's hands—the feel of moist clay upon eyes which have never seen, which perhaps had not even been perfectly formed— then the quiet command: "Go wash in the pool of Siloam."

The Blind Man's Faith

The man himself is a bit of a miracle. He does not remark on the unlikelihood of any healing properties being in the well-known pool, into which from boyhood days he may often have dipped his hands. He does not seem to think of the ridicule he will have to endure if no healing results from the washing; he does not murmur about the clay which is more suggestive of sealing up eyes than of opening them. He simply trusts the sound of that Voice and the touch of those hands, and he obeys. We follow him with the same breathless interest, as a friend or a disciple guides him to the pool, and curious skeptical onlookers crowd about him. We share his trembling expectancy as he stoops down, lifts the cool water in his hands, and bathes his eyes. Then, lo, he with his whole world is changed! Here is rapture that parallels the ecstacy of Saul Kane's new birth:

O glory of the lighted mind.
How dead I'd been, how dumb, how blind.
The station brook, to my new eyes,
Was babbling out of Paradise,
The waters rushing from the rain
Were singing Christ has risen again.
I thought all earthly creatures knelt
From rapture of the joy I felt.[1]

Yet St. John describes that gift of new vision in three words as quiet in their wonder as the waters of the pool of Siloam, "and came seeing." It is intriguing to wonder what was really the first thing that the man saw. The words of St. John seem to suggest that even in the rapture of that moment, when he found himself in an entirely new world of light and color and space, he hurried back, eager to see the face of Him whom he had known only through voice and hands and words.

Lesson of Sign—Necessity of New Vision

And now, from this radiant Sign of light that streams to us across the centuries, what lessons may we learn? First, it has something to say about the necessity of new vision. The word "vision" had become well-nigh obsolete in our mechanized world, but it is coming back into its own. There are three key texts that come to my mind whenever I think about that word of divine significance. "Where there is no vision, the people perish."[2] "I will pour out my spirit upon all flesh; and your sons and your daughters shall prophesy, your old men shall dream dreams, your young men shall see visions."[3] Then that heroic statement of faithfulness that towers above our feeble loyalties: "O king Agrippa, I was not disobedient unto the heavenly vision."[4] On the birthday of the Christian

[1]From *The Everlasting Mercy.* Copyright, 1911 by John Masefield. Used by permission of The MacMillan Company, publishers.
[2]Prov. 29:18.
[3]Joel 2:28.
[4]Acts 26:19.

Church Peter saw in the amazing experience of that hour the fulfilment of Joel's prophecy concerning spiritual illumination. This has significance for all who are members of that Church.

We know that Joel wrote his book at a time of great national calamity (probably around 500 B.C.) when the entire land of Judah was being devastated by locusts and drought. These grim enemies had often struck at the resources of the nation, causing suffering and death. But never had there been any visitation comparable in agony to the one he records: no food for man or beast; poor and wealthy alike experiencing the pangs of starvation, for there was no food for money to buy; and even the temple services discontinued, because there were no offerings of field or flock to bring to Jehovah. But the prophet in his clear vision sees the double calamity as God's judgment on the sin of the nation—the locusts and drought are instruments of Jehovah's wrath. There is, however, a way out—and history has proved that it is still the only way of survival—the whole nation must repent, a corporate repentance: "Rend your heart, and not your garments, and turn unto the Lord your God: for He is gracious and merciful."[1] The people obey, and God with an overflowing measure of mercy answers their prayer. He promises to remove the plagues and to restore fertility to the parched earth, so that it may bring forth an abundant harvest. But over and above this material restoration, He promises to pour out upon them the indispensable blessing of spiritual illumination and to cause "all flesh"—age and youth alike—to share in a nation-wide enlightenment.

Pattern of Illumination

This inner illumination which results from the action of the Holy Spirit in our individual hearts is the new vision that we who would walk in newness of life must have if we

[1]Joel 2:13.

are not to perish. It is the gift of "New Eyes for Invisibles," to use the title of a most timely book by Rufus Jones. New eyes will enable us to see not only the things relating to our earth-life, but also the eternal things which our natural vision cannot see. And the first thing this new sight does for us is show us the part we play in God's plan. The true pattern of religious illumination is given us in the call of Isaiah. Nowhere have I read a clearer setting forth of that pattern than in the chapter "The Mysticism of Isaiah,"[1] in *Art and Religion,* by Von Ogden Vogt. He enumerates the five progressive steps of the experience: *vision, humility, vitality, illumination, enlistment,* and shows how each step leads naturally to the next.

A vision of great beauty breaks in upon our souls, and— no matter what the initial cause:

> ...a sunset touch,
> A fancy from a flower-bell, some one's death,
> A chorus-ending from Euripides,[2]

or a national calamity, such as the one that compelled Isaiah to seek God in the temple—we are passive before this vision, as before great drama, great music, or great art.

As we gaze, the wonder and beauty and immensity of the vision make us suddenly humble. Each heart in its own words utters its "woe is me."

But even as we confess our inadequacy, a swift quickening begins within us. The vision, no longer aloof—although still "high and lifted up"—seems to be touching us intimately, and in that "flame of living love" our woe becomes vitality. We know now that we have a share in that beauty. We can in our own small way fashion ourselves after the pattern that has been shown us. We are not, of course, so great as that which we behold, but our finite faculties, cleansed and

[1]Von Ogden Vogt, *Art and Religion* (New Haven: Yale University Press, 1921), p. 145.

[2]Robert Browning, "Bishop Blougram's Apology," *Browning's Complete Poetical Works* (Boston: Houghton Mifflin and Company, 1895), p. 351. Used by permission.

kindled with the live coal from the altar, can contribute by reflecting some aspect of the Eternal Beauty in our lives.

And now our one desire is to abide with this vision, "to behold the beauty of the Lord"[1] and dwell in His house for evermore. But this vitality which has brought us a sense of power and worth will permit no such selfish enjoyment. The needs of others press in upon us. Like the monk in Longfellow's "The Legend Beautiful," who is summoned from his rapt enjoyment of the Presence of his Savior to feed the hungry poor, we must lose ourselves in the service of others. The Most High needs stewards to dispense His bounty to His needy children: "Whom shall I send, and who will go for us?"[2] There is no compulsion, save that which comes from the fervency of our love for Him who calls. So even at the cost of losing forever the precious contemplation of Beauty, we offer ourselves for enlistment in the only service that is perfect freedom: "Here am I; send me." Then, but not till then, do we realize that our self-offering has made the vision a permanent beatitude in our lives:

> Hadst thou stayed, I must have fled!
> This is what the vision said.[3]

Enlargement of Vision

As we look back over these Signs, we see that each one has been leading us onward toward illumination. The enrichment which the first Sign brought aroused a concern for our family. Now we are realizing that His family is ours and includes the whole earth. The spirit of Jesus is permeating us—making us less concerned about ourselves, our comfort, our private enterprises. We are learning that the measure

[1]Ps. 27:4.

[2]Isa. 6:8.

[3]Henry W. Longfellow, "The Legend Beautiful," from "Tales of a Wayside Inn," *Longfellow's Poems* (Boston: Houghton Mifflin and Company, 1894).

of our worth lies in our dealings with others.

We are growing more sensitive to the leading of the Holy Spirit within and are caring less for the ridicule or criticism that obedience to His voice often brings. We try in our growing consideration for others to imitate—in the words of St. Francis of Assisi—"the courteous sky shining upon the just and unjust alike." At times the leading of the Spirit is more definite than at others. The important thing is that we be sensitive and obey promptly.

I remember a few years ago hurrying to a supper appointment. As I waited at the street corner for the light to change, an old woman of foreign birth was asking directions from two workmen who could not understand what she wanted. She had evidently lost her way. I could not understand her, but she showed me an address on a piece of paper. I knew the street, which was several blocks away, and gave as clear directions as I could. She turned feebly and pathetically in the direction I had indicated. There was something so desolate and broken about her that, as I hurried on, I wished I were not pressed from time, so that I might see her on her way. Then suddenly, before I had reached the middle of the next block, I stopped as if rooted to the sidewalk. A voice within had spoken startling words: "I was lost and bewildered in the streets of New Haven, and you did little about it." Instantly I turned, with a little prayer for forgiveness in my heart, overtook the old woman, and said, "If you'll let me see the paper again, I'll go with you and find the place you want."

Obedience to New Vision

As a matter of fact, such experiences are signs of the passing of spiritual adolescence. We are taking on the responsibilities and attitudes of adult life, a more whole-hearted dedication to our Father's business. New duties, new loyalties arise which test our obedience to this gift of new sight. We are following humbly in the footsteps of the Master who, as He passed, always helped individuals, no matter what the cost to His own plans. Our path is the path of unquestioning obedience. The blind man may have expected his sight to be restored instantly, but he had to wait and obey, and we must be willing to follow his example. After he had received his sight, his allegiance to Jesus caused him to suffer. He was excommunicated—shut out from the Temple. But his bravery and his loyalty never wavered. He did not act toward Jesus as the Israelites had acted toward Moses. He never once said, "Why did this man bring all this trouble upon me? Better had he left me at the Temple gates blind and begging; for then kind passers-by gave me alms, but now I am shut out of the religious fellowship of my people." He was no weakling. He was eager to shoulder the responsibilities and tackle the hardships that new sight brings. He saw, too, that the way of growth is the way of suffering.

But I think that the tenderest lesson taught us in this Sign is that Jesus enters our lives so simply:

> I come in the little things,
> Saith the Lord:[1]

Our ordinary and commonplace lives in their familiar, routine events offer all the opportunities we need for meeting with Jesus and learning of Him so that we may grow more like Him. Prophets who proclaimed Him and those who walked with Him did not compare Him to a great river like the Euphrates, changing by the pressure of its mighty waters the contour of the plain through which it flows; they likened Him to the gentle, unobtrusive "waters of Shiloah that go softly."[2]

---

[1]Evelyn Underhill, from "Immanence," *Immanence, a Book of English Verses* (London: J. M. Dent and Sons, Ltd., 1914), p. 1.

[2]Isa. 8:6.

Transforming Effect of Vision

This tender, quiet coming of our God into our lives is the way of transformation. As with the blind man, there is something so different about us after we have received new sight that many who knew us before the experience doubt if we are the same persons. The truth is that we are the same, yet not the same. "I live; yet not I, but Christ liveth in me."[1] We have seen the King in His beauty, and that impact with the "Beauty of ancient days" is having a sacramental effect on our lives.

Moses never forgot the "good will of Him that dwelt in the bush."[2] Ingratitude, abuse, disloyalty—all the desperate hardship and disillusionment of that forty years' struggle toward the Promised Land—nothing could dim the vision of the burning bush. He could close his eyes in the early morning, in the blazing noontide, or late at night, and there it was, shining steadily, a permanent vision. Jeremiah never forgot the dark branch of the almond tree blown into starry whiteness by the stirring of spring. That vision of creative beauty stayed before his eyes and, even in the foul mire of a dungeon, spoke ever the same message, assuring him that "He that keepeth Israel" is always awake and aware. And St. Paul, when he had received new sight, in the glorious vision of all, rejoiced that he was held fast forever in the "trailing clouds of glory" that had fallen about him on the Damascus road. In tribulation, in suffering, in death, that vision of beauty endured before his eyes—the shining symbol of One who was a light about his feet and who was acquainted with all his ways.

[1]Gal. 2:20.
[2]Deut. 33:16.

Keeping the Vision Clear

Now let us consider some practical suggestions to aid us in keeping our new vision clear. That wondrous sixteenth century saint, Teresa of Avila, who belongs to all whose single desire is to see the King in His beauty, writes much that is helpful in her *Interior Castle and Mansions,* the book which completes her great trilogy on the spiritual life. She describes how she had a vision of "a most beautiful gold crystal like a castle" of seven mansions, and in the seventh and central one the King of Glory had His shining throne. The light of His Presence illumined all the other mansions as well as all the dwellings outside the castle walls; but those who dwelt nearest the central mansion received the greatest illumination.

Room of Intellect

Our complex mind is an "interior castle"; and clarity of sight depends upon the cleansing and reordering of its many rooms. We feel with Evelyn Underhill that St. Paul's "temple" and St. Teresa's "castle" are far too exalted ideals for the feeble "called-to-be saints" that we are. Even her lowlier term "house" does not come down to our level. "Cottage" seems more suited to our aspirings. But "castle" does have valid connotations: great entrances (the five senses); vast rooms (the faculties of mind); and a dark underground dungeon (the subconscious) of which psychology has made us aware. Let us look at the rooms, their connecting doors slightly ajar, for no faculty is complete in itself and each is connected with the dungeon by a trapdoor hinged so that it opens from below. Let us visit, in our limited time, the more important rooms. Here is the room of the intellect, that marvelous "brain force" which God has given us with no restrictions whatsoever upon our use of it. The great misuse of the intellect is pride. I think Southey spoke of "the march of the intellect" proceeding at quick time. Today he would say "double quick," even " 'blitz' quick," we fear. It was a poet, James Russell Lowell, and not a minister, who warned us that "the intellect has only one failing.... It has no conscience." This forward march means only disaster, unless it is directed by God. We must fling wide the doors of this room so that the light of Christ may flood every part of it. In those purifying rays all our preconceived ideas and wisdom—which is not wisdom at all—give place to the knowledge, wisdom, and understanding which are part of the sevenfold gift of the Holy Spirit. Then our "I know" will become "Thou knowest."

Room of Memory

Next we enter the great chamber of the memory, the "immeasurable capacity" of which moved St. Augustine to say: "Great is this force of memory, excessive great, O my God; a large and boundless chamber! Who ever sounded the bottom thereof?"[1] This vast room, the storehouse of "all that is past," is packed with everything that we have heard or seen or read or thought or done—all the "so much bad in the best of us" and the "so much good in the worst of us"— all the "old, unhappy, far-off things, and battles long ago." The light of Christ must flood this room also, and in this light we must set it in order. Valueless and disturbing and harmful memories must be blotted out; and only those necessary for growth in newness of life retained.

What a beautiful room it now becomes! Here we meet again all the good, glad, selfless ones who shaped our lives; all the natural beauty of field and forest, mountain, sea, and sky; all cherished events that made our journey a "more golden way" and—most precious of all God's gifts to us— the records of His mercy and goodness. As the light of His love fills the room, it consumes all those memories of uncharitableness that cling to us like burs—the wrongs we did to others and the wrongs others did to us. All the heartbreaking

[1] *The Confessions of St. Augustine, op. cit., p. 212.*

108

recollection of sins, long since repented of and forgiven, which we find so hard to forget, although He remembers them no more—all these are blotted out in the light and love of His abiding.

Room of Imagination

We pass on to the room of the imagination—"so full of shapes," that "splendid and dangerous faculty" that gives form and color to our thoughts and desires. Ezekiel saw the tragedies that resulted from the misuse of these "dark chambers of imagery" in which wrong thoughts and desires are painted in such appealing colors and shapes that the will, stirred to action by their false beauty, converts them into sinful deeds. This dangerous use of so valuable a faculty must cease, and its splendid use be nurtured. In the light and guidance of the Holy Spirit, it can be cleansed and consecrated and taught to create images that make for holiness. These images must be made so truly beautiful that they will compel the will, swiftly and joyously, to convert them in those "deeds of love and mercy" that mark the heavenly kingdom. Then—most splendid transformation of all—this illumined imagination will gradually take on the nature of a mirror in which at all times we may behold the glory of the face of Jesus Christ, and, little by little, by keeping our eyes steadfastly on "that one face," we shall be changed into His likeness.

Room of Will

And now we enter the most important chamber, the great room of the will, that "relentless drive of our nature" which reveals the true condition of our "interior castle," for it converts into deeds all that we think or remember or imagine or desire. This marvelous will, our share in the creative energy of God, was purposely given to us free, so that we might be sons and not puppets. It must be cleansed, and so permeated with "that most excellent gift of charity, the very bond of peace and of all virtues,"[1] that it will obey only the impulse of love. "Love, and do what you please" is St. Augustine's classic summary of the spiritual life.

Ian Maclaren, in one of his charming stories, says, " 'I will' is no word for a man. There is a far diviner one—'I ought.' " This will, cleansed and consecrated, will draw all our faculties away from the things they naturally desire, and center them in unified strength upon God. This action— of invaluable use in prayer—is called recollection. It must be assiduously practiced if our prayer-life is to be fruitful.

What an exalted service is this to which new vision calls us! We are to be stewards of light and water to a needy world. Like Ezekiel, in the Valley of Vision, we must cry in simple faith: "Come from the four winds,[1] O Holy Spirit, and breathe upon us that we may live! Enter our interior castle and breathe through every faculty of sense and mind thy purifying, quickening power. Consecrate completely our entire being so that 'at all times and in all places' we may reflect the grace and power and loveliness of Jesus. And in Thy tender mercy, keep our vision undimmed so that 'Whereas I was blind, now I see' may be the glad certainty of our lives."

[1] Ezek. 37:9.

Chapter Seven

Maturity

John 11:18-44
The Raising of Lazarus

Now Bethany was nigh unto Jerusalem, about fifteen furlongs off: and many of the Jews came to Martha and Mary, to comfort them concerning their brother. Then Martha, as soon as she heard that Jesus was coming, went and met him: but Mary sat *still* in the house. Then said Martha unto Jesus, Lord, if thou hadst been here, my brother had not died. But I know, that even now, whatsoever thou wilt ask of God, God will give *it* thee. Jesus saith unto her, Thy brother shall rise again. Martha saith unto Him, I know that he shall rise again in the resurrection in the last day. Jesus said unto her, I am the resurrection, and the life: he that believeth in Me, though he were dead, yet shall he live: and whosoever liveth and believeth in Me shall never die. Believest thou this? She saith unto Him, Yea, Lord: I believe that thou art the Christ, the Son of God, which should come into the world. And when she had so said, she went her way, and called Mary her sister secretly, saying, the Master is come, and calleth for thee. As soon as she heard *that,* she arose quickly, and came unto Him. Now Jesus was not yet come into the town, but was in that place where Martha met Him. The Jews then which were with her in the house, and comforted her, when they saw Mary, that she rose up hastily and went out, followed her, saying, She goeth unto the grave to weep there. Then when Mary was come where Jesus was, and saw Him, she fell down at His feet, saying unto Him, Lord, if thou hadst been here, my brother had not died. When Jesus therefore saw her weeping, and the Jews also weeping which came with her, He groaned in the spirit, and was troubled, and said, Where have ye laid him? They said unto Him, Lord, come and see. Jesus wept. Then said the Jews, Behold how He loved him! And some of them said, Could not this man, which opened the eyes of the blind, have caused even this man should not have died? Jesus therefore again groaning in Himself cometh to the grave. It was a cave, and a stone lay upon it. Jesus said, Take ye away the stone. Martha, the sister of him that was dead, saith unto Him, Lord, by this time he stinketh; for he hath been *dead* four days. Jesus saith unto her, Said I not unto thee, that, if thou wouldest believe, thou shouldest see the glory of God? Then they took away the stone *from the place* where the dead was laid. And Jesus lifted up *His* eyes, and said, Father, I thank thee that thou hast heard me. And I knew that thou hearest me always: but because of the people which stand by I said *it,* that they may believe that thou hast sent me. And when He thus had spoken, He cried with a loud voice, Lazarus, come forth. And he that was dead came forth, bound hand and foot with gravecloths: and his face was bound about with a napkin. Jesus saith unto them, Loose him, and let him go.

With inspired certainty of heart and mind St. John had led us from Sign to Sign up to the wondrous seventh, "The Raising of Lazarus," which completes and crowns, as with a royal diadem, the public ministry of Jesus. Well might St. Chrysostom say: "St. John made ready his soul as some well-fashioned and jeweled lyre with strings of gold, and then yielded it to the Holy Spirit for the utterance of something great and sublime." Through six vivid scenes we have watched the incomparable Savior manifesting in time His divine authority and kingly glory in order that we, seeing that glory and admitting that authority, "may believe that Jesus is the Christ, the Son of God, and believing may have life through His Name."[1] Such revelation of the will of God for us is too wonderful; we cannot attain to it. The Lord of life lays aside His glory, takes our flesh upon Him, and dwells among us, intent upon one glorious end—our eternal life: "Because I live, ye shall live also."[2]

From earliest ages an insatiable hunger in the heart of man for more abundant life has led him to conceive of gods who would visit men, but how different was the motive that brought such gods to earth from that which moved "the Dayspring from on high" to visit us! In Norse mythology, Odin, the All-Father, disguised as a wanderer, lives for a while among men, and sacrifices his right eye for a drink from the Well of Wisdom in order to help them more wisely. It is a moving story, suggestive of the upward groping of the human soul toward the light of the sublime reality of Emmanuel, "God with us," not merely to visit and to aid, but to die so that mankind may live.

Throughout St. John's Gospel there is that nonhuman blend of power and love, almighty and most merciful, that shines forth in every Sign and reveals the nature of God. We

[1]John 20:31. From *The Bible: A New Translation,* by James Moffatt, copyrighted by Harper [7] Bros., 1935. Used by permission.
[2]John 14:19.

see the Creator who is also the Father. Such love must eventually draw us home no matter how far we stray.

> 'The very God! think Abib; dost thou think?
> So, the All-Great, were the All-Loving too—'[1]

that is the atmosphere of wonder and of awe which the seventh Sign creates.

Jesus the Life of Men

The Raising of Lazarus is the culmination of all that St. John records in the first ten chapters of his Gospel about Jesus as the life of men. At the very outset he states this truth in words of simple grandeur: "In Him was life; and the life was the light of men."[2] But cold hearts, dull ears, dim eyes, and dark minds are unreceptive to light and life, and the message does not break through to the consciousness of those to whom it was uttered. The truth has to be announced over and over again. So, in chapter after chapter, St. John shows the Lord of Life and Light repeating and expounding the fact that the Son has eternal life for all, and that those who will accept it in Him shall live forever. Let us notice the frequent repetitions: Now the truth is told to Nicodemus, the honest though timid Rabbi: "He that believeth on the Son hath everlasting life...."[3] Now it is unfolded to the woman of Samaria whose home life is being exposed to the piercing and purifying rays of truth: "If thou knowest the gift of God, and Who it is that saith to thee, Give Me to drink; thou wouldest have asked of Him, and He would have given thee living water."[4] "The water that I shall give him shall be in him a well of water springing up into everlasting life."[5] Now, in the midst of bitter controversy, He is repeating the truth

[1]Robert Browning, "An Epistle," *Browning's Complete Poetical Works, op. cit.*, p. 340.
[2]John 1:4.
[3]John 3:36.
[4]John 4:10.
[5]John 4:14.

to His adversaries in words of solemn certitude: "He that heareth My word, and believeth on Him that sent Me, hath everlasting life."[1] "For the hour is coming, in the which all that are in the graves shall hear His voice, and shall come forth."[2] "Verily, verily, I say unto you, If a man keep My saying, he shall never see death."[3] "And I give unto them eternal life; and they shall never perish, neither shall any man pluck them out of My hand."[4] And finally, in the triumphant seventh Sign, He sums up for the comforting of Martha, and of those who love and believe on Him throughout the ages, His previous statements in rare words of beauty and power: "I am the resurrection, and the life: He that believeth in Me, though he were dead, yet shall he live: And whosoever liveth and believeth in Me shall never die."[5] The Church has placed these words of "sublime and awful beauty" at the beginning of the service for the burial of the dead. They fall upon our ears like trumpet notes sounded "from the hid battlements of Eternity"; and their compassionate authority, reminiscent of "It is I; be not afraid,"[6] brings comfort to all believers who mourn their "so-called dead."

Events Leading to Sign

Let us consider the remarkable events that lead up to this Sign. After the controversy resulting from the healing of the man born blind, the crowd becomes more and more perplexed and divided in their estimate of Jesus. The religious leaders grow alarmingly hostile, and because the man bravely persists in his defense of Jesus, they cast him out of the Temple. Jesus finds him, and step by step leads him to a firm belief in Him as the Christ of God.

[1]John 5:24.
[2]John 5:28, 29, 40.
[3]John 8:51.
[4]John 10:28.
[5]John 11:25, 26.
[6]John 6:20.

The casting out of the man gives rise to two great parables that reveal Jesus as Door and Shepherd. These in turn lead up to a definite statement of His death and resurrection. He makes it quite clear, however, that His death will be brought about neither by the treachery of a disciple nor by the plotting of His enemies. He lays His life down of Himself, and of Himself will take it again. Sir Edwin Hoskyns says: "His death...was the climax of Divine necessity, and His whole life and ministry moved steadily towards it...."[1] The compulsion to die was the compulsion which His love for sinners laid upon Him—that "love of Christ, which passeth knowledge," the "breadth, and length, and depth, and height" of which are so far beyond our comprehension.

A Yale professor once told me that William Blake's poem, "The Lamb," always brought a lump to his throat. It is this "Love that passeth knowledge" speaking through the poet's words that moves one so deeply. Christina Rossetti's poem, "Rejoice With Me," has the same quality:

> "Little Lamb, who lost thee?"
> "I myself, none other."
> "Little Lamb, who found thee?"
> "Jesus, Shepherd, Brother."[2]

And yet the compassionate words spoken by the Good Shepherd Himself, revealing His will to lay down His life for His sheep, fall on hard hearts and meet with derision: "He hath a devil, and is mad; why hear ye him?"[3] And Jesus withdraws.

Most commentators think that some weeks elapse before the Feast of the Dedication, when Jesus again appears in the Temple and teaches in Solomon's porch. This was a winter feast, appointed by Judas Maccabaeus for the annual commemoration of God's last great deliverance of the Jewish

---

[1]Sir Edwin Hoskyns, *The Fourth Gospel, op. cit.*, p. 379.
[2]Christina G. Rossetti, "Rejoice With Me," *Poetical Works* (New York: The Macmillan Company).
[3]John 10:20.

116

nation. On the 25th of December, 168 B.C., Antiochus Epiphanes, king of Syria, in a determined attempt to stamp out the Hebrew religion, had desecrated the Temple and had set up an altar to the Greek god Zeus on the altar of burnt-offering. The horror of the situation brought forth heroic action, and the priestly family of the Maccabees, consisting of a father and five sons, led a resistance that has no parallel in Hebrew history. So completely did they throw off the yoke of Syria that Israel regained its independence, which it retained for nearly a hundred years. So decisive was the victory that on the third anniversary of the desecration—on the very same day, December 25—the Temple was repaired and purified and the regular services restored.[1]

Thus the Feast of the Dedication was a most appropriate time for our Lord's final appearance in His Father's house, and for His declaration of Himself as the Son, sanctified by the Father, and sent into the world as His Father's divine representative.[2] With characteristic penetration the author of the Fourth Gospel, describing the occasion, says simply: "And it was winter," for he sees in the time of year a symbol of the bleaker winter of unbelief which holds no promise of springtime quickening. The religious leaders surround Jesus and demand that He tell them plainly if He is the Christ. For nearly three years Jesus has been declaring that fact in word and deed, but they have refused to hear or to see. Yet, in words of singular tenderness, He again speaks of the Father's love and concern for the safety of the sheep: "No man is able to pluck them out of My Father's hand." And, finally, in brief words of sublime beauty, reminiscent of the verse with which the Fourth Gospel begins, He proclaims His essential oneness with the Father: "I and My Father are one," and calls upon His listeners to see in His works the truth of His words: "The Father is in Me and I in Him."

[1]Cf. I Maccabees 4:34-59; II Maccabees 1-2:18; 10:1-8.
[2]Cf. John 10:36.

To the Jews such a claim is blasphemous. They attempt to stone Him, but His appeal to His works and to the Old Testament restrains them. They plan His arrest, however. Jesus therefore leaves the Temple and Jerusalem and Judaea to the icy darkness of their spiritual winter and retires beyond the Jordan, for the "hour" is not yet.

It is in keeping with the whole theme of the Fourth Gospel that the closing scene of the public ministry of Jesus in Jerusalem should end with a declaration from His lips that He is the Son sanctified by the Father. The words immediately take us back in thought to His baptism: "This is My beloved Son, in whom I am well pleased."[1] And St. John goes on to record that Jesus, after His rejection in Jerusalem, returns to the place of His baptism where the Father had publicly acknowledged Him and where the Baptist had borne witness that He was the Lamb of God and the Son of God—the Sent One, who takes away sin and baptizes with eternal life. St. John draws a veil of tender reticence over all that the return to that hallowed spot meant to our Lord. He merely emphasizes the fact with an exactness that makes his words, "the place where John first baptized," throb with deep meaning. But oh, the golden wonder of that revisiting! Jesus finds that the Baptist's testimony has not been forgotten; people are still eagerly declaring that all that John had said about Him is true; and "many believed on Him there." We can almost see St. John underscoring *there*—that place of illumination and joyous commissioning, where he too had seen the Lord of Life for the first time.

Joyous Gospel Scenes

In the Gospels we happen now and then upon scenes so joyous that they draw us back again and again to linger and to give thanks. They admit us to the glad company of those

[1] Matt. 3:17.

118

who expressed their devotion to Jesus in tender deeds, seeking, as it were, to make amends for the heartbreak caused by the many who rejected His gift of new life. How grateful we are for St. Luke's record of the group of faithful and generous women who accompanied Jesus on His tours, looking out for His comfort in kindly unobtrusive ways and providing the means for His daily livelihood! Dr. F. Warburton Lewis makes them very real to us:

> Women of standing and honour and noble mind, led by the great Magdalene; women, these, who are the precursors of all who have supported the word of God by their liberality in every age and every church.... It is better to choose with Magdalene and Joanna and Susanna, and put our substance at His disposal;.... They who build for comfort in Capernaum are lost amid the dust of oblivion, but Magdalene and Susanna and Joanna are the first names of a great company among us for evermore.[1]

Then that blessed home in Bethany where Jesus was so beloved—sisters and brother knit together in devotion to Him. All friendship is dearer and purer and more unselfish because of that home. Our hearts go out to all three, but especially to Mary, whose "eyes are homes of silent prayer." She sensed what even His closest disciples could not grasp, and poured out her reverent devotion in a costly anointing, the fragrance of which still fills every home where Jesus is loved.

Then those last days of glad ministry near the scene of His baptism, spent in the company of those who remembered and believed and loved. Those happy days must have been followed by precious nights of communion with His Father.

[1]F. Warburton Lewis, *Jesus of Galilee* (London: Ivor Nicholson and Watson, 1931), p. 87. Used by permission of the author.

Surely it is not amiss to believe that that place of "revelation and wonder" witnessed an experience more intimate and more wondrous than that seen by Moses and Elias and the intimate three—as in tenderest love the Father flung wide the everlasting doors of His glory and

> ...on the Son
> Blaz'd forth unclouded Deity.[1]

But the days of fruitful ministry and hallowed communion had come to an end. The scene is set for the seventh Sign. A message comes to Jesus from Martha and Mary concerning their brother Lazarus: "Lord, he whom thou lovest is sick." The tender brief statement expresses a confidence that recalls the words of the mother of Jesus in the first Sign: "Whatsoever He saith unto you, do it." The sisters know that they can trust the wisdom and love of Jesus. He sends them a reply to the effect that their brother's sickness will not end in death, but is "for the glory of God, that the Son of God might be glorified thereby." It is a puzzling message, containing hope and comfort, yet calling for patience and trust. The Master is helping His dearest human friends to stretch up higher reaches of faith. He stays where He is for two days. He knows His delay will cause bewilderment and grief, but the delays and the silences of God have to be experienced and trusted if faith is to grow. Those who turn to God for help must never forget that He can "be still and look on" in His place, while He directs for our highest good everything that concerns us. The two days pass, and then in words that suggest a serene power moving toward a mighty manifestation, Jesus says to His disciples, "Let us go into Judaea again." Judaea! That name means danger and death; so the perplexed disciples express their concern for His safety. They have not yet learned that danger and death can have no power over Him unless it be given them from on

[1]John Milton, *Paradise Lost,* Bk. X.

high. The Master explains that Lazarus is dead and that He is going to awaken him, and filled with a sense of impending doom, the disciples resolve to go with Him. Again we note the striking contrast—illustrated in the second Sign—between the divine and human outlook. Jesus is speaking of the reality of life: "I go, that I may awake him out of sleep." The disciples are seeing death as the grim reality: "Let us also go, that we may die with Him."

Trust in Jesus Rewarded

As Jesus draws near to Bethany, a village two miles from Jerusalem on the eastern slope of the Mount of Olives and on the road to Jericho, Martha hurries out to meet Him with news that confirms what He has said to the disciples. Lazarus is dead, and has been four days buried. She knows that Jesus could have prevented the death had He been there, and feels that He can do something even now to help. She thinks, perhaps, that like the prophets of old He can pray to God and thus have Lazarus restored. Jesus startles her with a statement that glows like a flame through the gospel pages: "I am the resurrection and the life." He Himself is the source and fount of life. He is not like Elijah, who needed help in his work of quickening. He seems to say, "Martha, Martha, do you believe that I, your friend and teacher, am very God, holding the keys of death and the grave in My hands?"[1] Of course she does not grasp it all; yet something in these words of strange power makes her hurry back to the house to greet her sister with words of exquisite tenderness, that we should learn to listen for in our hours of grief: "The Master is come, and calleth for thee." Mary hastens to Him, and the Jews who have come to comfort the sisters (some of the bitterest enemies of the Master among them, as the cautious movements of the sisters seem to indicate) think that she is going to the

[1]Cf. J. C. Ryle, *Expository Thoughts on the Gospels*, Vol. II, pp. 264, 265.

grave, and follow her. When she sees Jesus, she falls at His feet weeping, and says the words that Martha and she have been repeating during those sorrowful four days: "Lord, if Thou hadst been here, my brother had not died." Her words are wiser than she knows, for "where Jesus is there can be no death." Her sorrow and the weeping of her friends move Jesus deeply. St. John uses strange words here. He tells us that Jesus "groaned in the spirit, and was troubled." The Greek word translated "groaned" means more anger than sorrow—and we can but feel, as some commentators do, that the emotion they describe is connected with the momentous Sign He is about to show forth. Some commentators believe that the words suggest an inner struggle with Satan, as Jesus, Lord of Life, is about to storm the last stronghold of the Prince of Darkness. Sir Edwin Hoskyns thinks that "the unbelief of the Jews and the half-belief of Martha and Mary" cause the disturbance of spirit that St. John records.[1] Followed by the crowd, Jesus moves toward the grave, shedding tears of human sympathy with His friends, a tender sharing of their grief that brings forth the observation from the Jews: "Behold how He loved him!" Standing before the grave, He orders the stone to be removed. Incredulous, yet expectant, Martha protests, then obeys. Facing the dark opening of the grave, Jesus lifts His eyes and prays to His Father using words that are more praise than prayer, and then cries with a loud voice, "Lazarus, come forth!" St. Augustine says that He called Lazarus by name, for had He not done so, all the dead would have arisen at that call. We can feel the hushed breathless moment that follows the summons of the Word "by whom all things were made." Then, the stirring within the tomb, and Lazarus, filled with such new life that even the grave-clothes do not prevent his walking, comes forth. Finally the quiet words of the Master fall like a benediction on a scene that holds in it the promise of an approaching Easter daybreak: "Loose him, and let him go."

[1]Cf. Sir Edwin Hoskyns, *The Fourth Gospel, op. cit.,* p. 405.

What This Sign Means

What does this Sign, the grandeur and importance of which cannot be estimated, mean to us? Every detail of the narrative has a message, but, since space is limited, we must content ourselves with the major lessons and try to apply them to our lives.

The first Sign took place in a home amid wedding festivities. But families have funerals as well as weddings, and it is no mere coincidence that the last, and greatest of the seven, also has a family setting. Jesus is, however, a beloved friend of every member of this family, and brings enrichment not by turning water into wine, but by turning death into life.

The fourth Sign, Sustenance, made us feel as though we were standing on holy ground. The seventh takes us into a Holy of Holies. In a special way it is our Sign. Let doubters reason as they will, they cannot take from us a Sign that in every glowing word tells of the Savior's love and might. The preceding Signs may seem remote in part from everyday experience. Not all of us have shared in the festive responsibilities of a wedding; wine may even be beyond our means, and so we have to interpret the Sign to fit our more frugal living.

Dr. Arthur J. Gossip tells of a Yorkshire miner who, having been converted, was tested by his fellows: "You don't really believe that yarn about Jesus turning the water into wine; do you?" The miner replied: " I am an ignorant man; I know nothing about water and wine. But I know this—that in my home Jesus Christ has turned beer into furniture! And that is a good enough miracle for me!"[1] That is the sort of experience that shows these Signs to have creative power in our lives. Some of us may never have sought Jesus on behalf of a dying child; may never have had a bodily infirmity from which we longed to be freed; may never have known the pangs of hunger; may never have lost our bearings amid

[1]Arthur John Gossip, *Experience Worketh Hope* (New York: Charles Scribner's Sons, 1944), pp. 38, 39. Used by permission.

dark seas and contrary winds; may never have been conscious of our blinded sight—but death is a different matter. Its shadow lies upon our homes and hearts. We know the truth of Longfellow's words—even if we don't want to think about it:

> And our hearts, though stout and brave,
> Still, like muffled drums, are beating
> Funeral marches to the grave.[1]

Freedom From Fear of Death

But the fear of death loses its power when we stand before the empty tombs of Lazarus and Jesus. God in His overflowing bounty has given us two empty tombs, so that no trace of fear might linger in our hearts. Had Jesus not raised Lazarus, it might be natural enough for us to say in our hour of bereavement, "Yes, Jesus did rise from the dead, but He is very God as well as very man; what about me?" So our Savior, anticipating our every need, leads us to an altogether human tomb, and like a prelude to His own glorious human-divine resurrection, shows life triumphant over death in us also—if we believe in Him and abide in Him. When, therefore, the body of a loved one lies in the grave, we can open our Bible at this seventh Sign and find comfort in the experience of the family at Bethany. If we listen, the strong life-giving words of Jesus will fall also on our ears: "Thy mother, father, sister, brother, wife, husband, child, friend, shall rise again." And we know that we shall meet our loved one and recognize him in the radiance and perfection of his spiritual body. "I believe in the resurrection of the body" is the certainty that keeps us brave as we "wait awhile God's instant which men call years." Such faith gives us the power to see Death as the imposter that he is and to flout him in his face:

[1] Henry W. Longfellow, "A Psalm of Life," *Longfellow's Poems, op. cit.*

Death, be not proud, though some have called thee
Mighty and dreadful, for thou art not so:
For those whom thou thinkest thou dost overthrow
Die not, poor Death; nor yet canst thou kill me.[1]

That is the assurance which the early Christians had and which they passed on to us. They imitated Jesus by speaking of death as "a falling asleep." Even the word "cemetery" expresses their faith, for it means "a sleeping place." Eugene O'Neil's triumphant little play, "Lazarus Laughed," will, I believe, be read and treasured when many of his other plays are forgotten, for it has an eternal message based on this Sign. The theme of the play might well be summed up in words spoken by George Macdonald to one who was crushed by bereavement: "If you knew that God knows about death, you would clap your listless hands!"[2]

Jesus Vanquisher of Death

It is well to note that the Gospels record three specific times when Jesus raised people from the dead. Jairus' daughter had just died and was still on her bed. The son of the widow of Nain was already on the way to the grave. Had these two miracles alone been recorded, skeptics might well reason that Jesus had aroused the girl from unconsciousness and the boy from a prolonged coma. But the raising of Lazarus admits of no such explanation. Even our Lord's bitterest enemies did not question the miracle. It was the momentous fact that He had raised Lazarus, and by the sheer wonder of the deed had turned many of His enemies into believers, that made the authorities tremble for their own security and plan to put both Jesus and Lazarus to death.

[1] John Donne, "Death," from *Holy Sonnets.*
[2] C. S. Lewis, *George Macdonald, An Anthology* (New York: The Macmillan Company, 1947), p. 90.

Isaiah had foretold that the Messiah would "swallow up death in victory"—"annihilate" is the word used by one translator; and Hosea had revealed the same divine purpose: "I will ransom them from the power of the grave; I will redeem them from death: O death, I will be thy plagues; O grave, I will be thy destruction."[1] Jesus brought these prophecies to glorious fulfilment.

To all who seek to grow in newness of life He puts the same question that He put to Martha: "Believest thou this?" Do we really believe that if we have faith in Him, we partake of His life and shall never die? Are we confident that neither famine nor disease nor violent changes in the structure of our world nor atomic warfare—nothing can destroy those who are united with the life of Jesus? If we do not, we must ask Him to increase our faith until we do; for this glorious belief has made valiant saints from Martha's generation to ours. It is a mark of spiritual maturity to see the manifestation of God's glory in this seventh Sign. When we find in Jesus our resurrection and our life, Love is becoming victorious in our lives.

Marks of Spiritual Maturity

And now, how is this triumphant love, this mark of spiritual maturity, to find highest expression in our everyday living? Jesus calls us forth from our own narrow, unillumined selves as unmistakably as He called Lazarus forth from the grave. He sets our feet in a larger room. He wants us to be freed from the grave-clothes of old habits and old ideas, and He expects us to help one another in the loosening of the old bands. There can be no selfish advancement in newness of life. We must minister, as Jesus did, to the needs of others, and receive with gracious readiness any loving service offered to us. Strong in our resurrection powers, we must show by our actions that we are enrolled in the picked troops of God—a Gideonlike band pledged to the overthrow of evil and the triumph of

[1]Hos. 13:14.

126

good. The certainty that we are alive for evermore frees us from all fear of what may happen to us in our courageous consecration to our Father's business and in our filial resolve to make the life of Jesus our daily pattern.

John Wesley has given us a clear-cut measuring rod for testing the reality of our rebirth. Our answers to his questions reveal the degree of our maturity. 1. "Do you pray always?" 2. "Do you rejoice in God every moment?" 3. "Do you in everything give thanks?—in loss, in pain, in sickness, weariness, disappointments?" 4. "Do you desire nothing?" 5. "Do you fear nothing?" 6. "Do you feel the love of God continually in your heart?" 7. "Have you a witness in whatever you speak or do, that it is pleasing to God?"[1] Searching questions for self-examination, and yet John Wesley did not think that they cover all that is expected of a sanctified person! They certainly remind us that Jesus wants men, not weaklings, for the demands of the redemptive crusade in which we are enlisted are tremendous.

There can be no looking back on the old life of complaisant selfishness, if we are to inherit the Kingdom of God. The Cross is not a decorative emblem, but something on which our old self must be crucified, so that the words of St. Paul: "I live, yet not I," may have some measure of meaning for us also. But these seven Signs point no negative way to perfection. We are still to enjoy—and in a sense more deeply than ever— the beauty of our temporal world, but we are to see it as "the many-splendoured" garment of the Beauty of Ancient Days. Our love for family and friends becomes a foretaste of the "Love we just fall short of in all love," and our everyday tasks, the rich gifts of heart and mind and hand, and all noble achievement attained through years of faithful toil, do but anticipate the coveted "Well done" that will admit us into the joy of the Lord.

[1] *The Journal of John Wesley* (Everyman's Library Edition; New York E. P. Dutton & Co., Inc., 1906), Vol. I, p. 479. Used by permission.

Hindrances to Growth

Now let us relate the lessons of this seventh Sign to the Rule of Life that we have been developing. Chapter I stressed the nurture of obedience by means of family prayers and grace at meals. Chapter II added the daily habit of praise and thanksgiving. Chapter III called for Bible reading and emphasized the restorative power of forgiveness. Chapter IV led on to the practice of simple meditation. Chapter V encouraged the use of silence for listening and receiving. Chapter VI showed how to use the mind in recollection. And now Chapter VII presents the three major obligations that maturity brings: corporate worship, private worship, and intercession. The aim of a Rule of Life is to help us to become more Christlike. This is a fact that cannot be stressed too often. When we stand before the throne of God, we know perfectly well that the attendant angels will not whisper, "Isn't she a wonderful Baptist!" or "What a perfectly splendid Methodist!" or "What an outstanding Episcopalian!" The only thing that will really matter will be, can they look at us and then at one another and say reverently, "How like Jesus she is!" That is our single aim. But there are grave difficulties in the way when we set out to imitate Him. We speak of these difficulties as hindrances.

Olive Wyon, in her helpful book, *The School of Prayer,* has two excellent chapters on the fundamental and practical hindrances that beset our prayer life. The fundamental ones arise from our incorrect ideas about God and our lack of understanding of the true nature of prayer. The practical ones come from wandering thoughts, discouragement, dryness, daydreaming, and so on. The New Testament, however, reveals the threefold source of all difficulties that hinder spiritual growth— "the world, the flesh, and the devil." These names have become practically outmoded in an age that is more concerned with exterior than with interior warfare. But the realities abide—ignore or rename them as we please. Like the Ten Commandments they do not budge.

The World

What is the "world" but the "enemy without the gate"?—our absorption in *things*; the sin of putting other gods before our Heavenly Father; the worldly interests that choke the good seed; the commercialization that crowds out the true meaning of Christmas and Easter; our indifference to the disciplines of Advent and Lent; all the cheap jesting about spiritual things; the dragging of the name of Jesus into shallow conversations; the intellectual pride which does not bother to crucify Christ but just ignores Him. This is the "world" that hated Jesus. It is our enemy, too, for it deludes us into laying up our treasure for moth and rust and thieves.

The Flesh

What is the "flesh" but the "enemy within the gates"?—the "Old Adam" in us that resists goodness; the "other self" that is opposed to the things of God; our desire for ease; the hydra-headed egotism which is the deadliest of all sins: the self that works through all our senses to weaken or destroy our prayer life. To renounce the flesh does not mean to renounce our bodies. God created our bodies and pronounced them good. He gave us our senses as a part of a necessary equipment for our physical world. Jesus healed bodies and fed and refreshed them. But the flesh does become an enemy when it makes us forget that the body was created to be a temple of the Holy Ghost,[1] an "instrument of righteousness unto Him."[2] The New Testament teaches that it is our religious duty to care for our bodies. "Brother Ass," as St. Francis of Assisi lovingly called the body, is to be sancitfied, and we are to pray and work for its sanctification.

[1] I Cor. 6:19.
[2] Rom. 6:13.

The Devil

What of the devil?—that "master of the art of disturbing the soul"? Our fundamental hindrances all stem from him— the great usurper of the priority of God. He builds up in our minds false ideas about God; he sows doubts—not the honest questioning which is often the battleground where the spurs of faith are won, but the shallow doubt that questions only to overthrow our faith: "Does God really care for us? I shall never pray again because my prayers were not answered." All worry, fear, despondency, self-pity that result in enfeebled will—everything that keeps us from persevering in the way of newness of life has its origin in "the prince of this world."

Today these formidable adversaries have either been dismissed from our thoughts or so toned down that they seem quite harmless. The World and the Flesh are not so bad after all. Service to God and Mammon can be judiciously blended. And as for the Devil—except for C. S. Lewis, who has taken up the quarrel of Paul, Luther, Bunyan, and Wesley with "that ancient foe"—the Devil has become just an amusing person—if he is still permitted to be a person—who is to be appeased and joked about instead of being driven "from all his fortress stars," the way the early Church gave him battle.

The Way of Victory

But the fact remains that from these three comes everything that hinders our spiritual growth, and we need the whole armor of God for their vanquishing. In the Litany in the *Book of Common Prayer* there is a petition full of tenderness and deep wisdom for all who would walk in newness of life: "That it may please thee to strengthen such as do stand; and to comfort and help the weakhearted; and to raise up those who fall; and finally to beat down Satan under our feet." It seems to express perfectly the inadequacy we feel as we struggle with the unfathomable mystery of evil. A spiritual guide once told me that the wisest way to overcome hindrances to prayer is to turn them over, one by one as they arise, to the Holy Spirit, and by a sheer effort of the will to fix our minds on Jesus. We must absolutely refuse to let them baffle or worry us. All who have learned the power and wonder of prayer have had to overcome hindrances. Our victory lies in clinging to the Cross and refusing to let go, and in remembering that we pray to God who knows "that we have no power of ourselves to help ourselves."

Obligations

But the proof of victory in our spiritual life is not freedom from hindrances, but opportunities for service. As we grow in newness of life, our relationship to God becomes cumulative—servant, disciple, friend, son—but each advancing stage retains all the qualities and responsibilities of the earlier relationship. I like the word "servant." It is St. Paul's favorite word. In fact, he adds "bond" which makes it mean "slave." He rejoices that he has been bought like a slave by the blood of Jesus into a service that is perfect freedom. The old freedom to follow the inclinations of his heart is exchanged for the new freedom to serve and to love, to be servant and son, the twin words that sum up the mission of Jesus. In a similar way, newness of life makes us free so that we may fulfil the new obligations: corporate worship, private worship, and intercession.

Corporate Worship

The privilege of corporate worship is ours because we have been baptized into that glorious fellowship—the Church, founded by Jesus—a fellowship that is concerned with our entire life. We are baptized into its life, are sustained by its sacraments, and strengthened through its services. Week by week we join with others in rendering thanks for benefits received, in showing forth God's praise, in listening to His most holy Word, and in making known our needs of body and soul—and all this in the happy intimacy of one family in one Father's house. The Church is not a club, but a living Body into which we are built up. Each individual cell is of inestimable value, for it must share in and contribute to the life of the whole. To claim to be a Christian and neglect going to church is not the way the Bible teaches. The book of Acts reveals the importance of belonging to that holy fellowship which cannot be interrupted by death: "The Lord added to the church daily such as should be saved."[1]

But the Church is no exclusive, self-centered fellowship. It is deeply conscious of and lovingly concerned with the needs of the world. Its great insistence on almsgiving, prayer, and fasting bears witness to its unselfishness. Schools, hospitals, homes for children and for the aged, the great Christian social program of visiting the sick, feeding the hungry, clothing the naked, visiting the imprisoned—all the vast charities are summed up in the simple word, "to do good, and to distribute, forget not; for with such sacrifices God is well pleased."[2] These varied activities result from the new life that the Church nurtures in its members. To be a member of the Church is not merely a privilege; it is our very life, for the main business of the Church is our Father's business— our salvation.

Intercession

But the vitality of a body depends upon the vitality of each member. Therefore, the wholeness and richness of our corporate worship depend upon the private worship, the personal religion, and the prayer-life of each member. Our private worship has been set forth in the preceding chapters, but this seventh Sign, which marks our maturity, lays upon us the crowning privilege of intercession. Many excellent books on

[1] Acts 2:47.
[2] Heb. 13:16.

132

prayer contain definite instruction in the art of intercession, and each branch of the Church provides its own special aids for its members. I find *Instructions in the Life of Prayer,* by Charles F. Whiston, simple, thorough, and altogether practical.

One of the amazing facts of our faith is that Jesus "ever liveth to make intercession for us." If we truly love Him, that glorious fact alone should make intercession imperative. There is no joy comparable to that of offering ourselves to share in work that Jesus is endlessly doing *on our behalf.* If we are alive in Him, we must pray for others. A verse in Isaiah took on new and tremendous meaning some years ago when I read Professor Badè's comment on it: "Thy slain men are not slain with the sword, nor dead in battle."[1] These are almost the last public words spoken by the aged prophet as he watched the exultant crowds thronging the housetops and cheering madly for a victory that Isaiah well knew was no victory at all; for they had perfected all the material means of defense, with never a thought of God in their minds. "Such his [Isaiah's] living contemporaries never even tried to stand their ground in battle for prizes which are above comfort and above life."[2] We have come through a second world war, and it may well be that in the sight of God the dead are not those who have fallen on the various battle fronts. We who call ourselves the living may really be the dead, if the "desperate tides of the whole great world's anguish" do not move us to give fully and freely of our substance, our prayers, and ourselves. Can we not catch a vision of what it would mean if God could say of this great and fair land that knows nothing of the anguish of Europe and Asia: "I have set intercessors upon thy walls, O America; they shall never hold their peace day nor night: ye that are the Lord's remembrancers, take ye no rest and give Him no rest, till He establish, and

[1] Isa. 22:2.
[2] William F. Badè, *The Old Testament in the Light of Today, op. cit.,* pp. 185, 186.

till He make America a praise in the earth."[1] If this were so, there would be such an outpouring of blessing that, in the grand hyperbole of Malachi: "there shall not be room enough to receive it."[2]

Dynamic Prayer

Why do those who have proven the power of prayer plead so much for intercession? Why did Dr. E. Stanley Jones have yearly at his many ashrams unbroken intercession in twenty-four-hour periods? Why is there such a plea for prayer-cells and prayer-groups everywhere? Why are there societies that exist almost entirely for the work of intercession? Why are there many individuals, like Professor Charles F. Whiston, who make it their main business? It is because prayer is dynamic. It is the only force with power sufficient to shock evil from the earth. It is the only defense against the destructive use of atomic power. And if we care enough, we can make prayer the great force that it must be in our world if our civilization is to survive. We need—and the need is more urgent than we dare think—true peacemakers, a great mobilized army of the spiritually armed, who will dedicate themselves to forge on the anvils of prayer a lasting peace. Every church member should belong to a prayer-cell or a prayer-group and should set apart at least fifteen minutes every day for the task of intercession—and it is a task. It is being done by many—alas! too few! Everyone who has enough love for Jesus and enough love for humanity to dedicate himself or herself to a life of intercession will testify to the transformation that the very act of interceding brings about in the intercessor's life. It is a costly service, but the reward is beyond all price; and far from interfering with our daily tasks, it enhances them.

[1]Cf. Isa. 62:6, 7.
[2]Mal. 3:10.

In a Good Friday play, "The Rite of the Passion," by Charles Williams, the mother of Jesus turns to her son and says:

> O Son, long since in Cana at thy feast
> did I not turn to thee when the wine had ceased?
> but now I look on the whole world and see
> there is no wine anywhere nor any glee,
> but an end to feasting and an end to mirth
> and cruel habitations through the earth,
> and the mind unhappy and the soul undone;
> therefore now I cry again to thee, O Son,
> for entreaty, for a summons and a sign,
> O Love, O blessed Love, they have no wine![1]

In reply Jesus asks her if she realizes what the giving of wine to them will mean? It will end the happy companionship and home life that she and He have shared. His mother replies, "They have no wine." He presses the point still further, reminding her that He is the wine that must be poured out for their lack, and asks her if she knows the doom that fulfilling her summons will bring about. Still His mother's only answer is, "They have no wine."

Sacrificial Love

Can we even attempt to reach up to such sacrificial heights of love? We have witnessed these seven Signs. We are feeling their transforming power. We are under solemn obligation to turn to Jesus now with the same brief entreaty: "They have no wine." We must offer ourselves, at whatever cost, as channels of His life-giving power. We shall have to make a triple outpouring of almsgiving, prayer, and fasting. We must give freely so that others may have; we must live disciplined, controlled, temperate lives, offering ourselves as chalices—or cups, if we like the more homelike word—to be filled so that others may quench their thirst. This is maturity.

[1]Charles Williams, "The Rite of the Passion," *Three Plays* (New York: Oxford University Press, 1931), Part I, p. 147. Used by permission.

This is life. To say that we have no time for intercession is merely admitting that we do not care enough. We are the dead. One of the most helpful ways to intercede is to personalize the Lord's Prayer for an individual or for the world. The adaptation is simple. In his booklet, Professor Whiston presents it thus:

Our Heavenly Father:
Thy name be hallowed in (John) today;
Thy kingdom come in (John) today;
Thy will be done in (John) today;
As it is done in Thy heavens.
Give (John) today his daily bread;
Forgive (John) today his trespasses, and lead (John) to forgive all those who trespass against him today;
Lead (John) not into temptation today;
Deliver (John) today from all Evil.

We all have time to use it many times a day for individuals who are in any distress whatever. It has brought healing and peace and readjustment and mental stability to many, and has wrought miracles in some lives. Its daily use for the world would bring the same results. In Professor Whiston's booklet there is also an admirable list of essential daily intercessions. We should pray for our family, our friends, our bishop, our pastor, our parish; the rulers of the nations; special individuals whose needs have been brought to our notice; and for our enemies, private and national.[1] All for whom we pray should be mentioned by name.

The Way of Eternal Life

To help us to walk in newness of life is the aim of this book. We have seen in our study of the Signs of the Fourth Gospel how transformation begins and grows, step by step, until it

[1]Charles F. Whiston, *Instructions in the Life of Prayer* (Cincinnati: The Forward Movement) p. 10, *seq.* Temporarily out of print, but Forward Movement plans to republish in the future. Write them if you are interested.

reaches a deathless maturity, when we abide in Jesus and partake of His eternal life. But reading and study are not enough. We must do with these Signs what Keats suggested one should do with "a page of full Poesy or distilled prose." We must read them, wander with them, and muse upon them, and reflect from them, and bring home to them and prophesy upon them: until they become stale. But when will they do so? NEVER![1] These Signs must, through prayerful meditation, become our meat and drink day by day. The more receptive we are to the indwelling life of Jesus that is manifested in each Sign, the more sturdy will be our growth. Many years ago, in a little Lenten book, *The Return of God,* by Bede Frost, I came upon a paragraph of such exquisite beauty that I adapted it to my own need, memorized it, and have used it almost daily ever since. I pass it on, with further adaptations, to all who use this book, for its admonitions sum up perfectly the teachings of the seven Signs:

> Child of the Eternal Perfect, "loved with an everlasting love," created to be immortal and to be "filled with all the fulness of God," "let passing things pass." "Fix thine eyes upon the Eternal Beauty, cast thyself upon the Eternal Strength, dwell in the Eternal Life, rejoice in the Eternal Wisdom and Love," show forth thy Father's glory in a holy life of service, prayer, and praise, so shalt thou walk in newness of life, until thou come at last to that Eternal Beatitude which is God Himself.[2]

[1] Cf. John Keats, "Letter to Reynolds."
[2] Cf. Bede Frost, *The Return to God, op. cit.,* p. 68. Used by permission.

Suggestions for Study

Chapter One

New Birth

1. Dean Inge in *Personal Religion and the Life of Devotion* says "The doctrine of Christ as the living water runs through these chapters of St. John, recurring, like a musical phrase, in hints and symbolic language...."[1] Look up these references (chapters 1-7), and see how they meet vital needs in our spiritual lives.

2. What are the properties of water that make it a fit symbol for the Holy Spirit? What qualities are not applicable to God—but to man?

3. Read Chapters 1 and 2 in *The Royal Way of the Cross*[2] by Fénelon. Try to think of the aspect of God's richness which Jesus revealed.

4. Obedience is one of the first steps in a life of devotion. For fuller instruction in obedience, read the chapter on "Holy Obedience" in *A Testament of Devotion*[3] by Thomas R. Kelly.

5. What guidance do you find in this Sign in regard to (1) relations of children to parents and of parents to children; (2) pride in a family tree; (3) the old saying, "Noblesse oblige"?

6. What do you find in this miracle that bears similarity to that of the Healing of the Syrophoenician Woman's Daughter? (Matthew 15:21-28; Mark 7:24-30.)

---

[1]W. R. Inge, *Personal Religion and the Life of Devotion* (New York: Longmans, Green and Co., 12th Impression, 1937), p. 34.

[2]Francois de Salignac de la Mothe Fenelon, *The Royal Way of the Cross,* edited by Hal M. Helms; tr. by H. Sidney Lear (Paraclete Press, 1982), pp. 17-21.

[3]Thomas R. Kelly, *A Testament of Devotion* (New York: Harper & Bros., 1941), pp. 51-76.

7. Jesus enriches us by changing us. What types of people did He particularly try to change during His earthly ministry? What major changes must take place in us when we become His disciples? Give concrete examples from the New Testament of changed lives. What of changed lives today?

8. Jesus had performed no miracle before this one in Cana of Galilee. Can you, in reading the story of His life up to this point, find any reasons why His mother might expect Him to do something great at her request?

9. Make a comparative study of the occasions in the Gospels when parents appealed to Jesus on behalf of their children. Have you any suggestions to offer as to why there is no record of a child coming on behalf of a parent?

10. This miracle was a creative act on the part of Jesus. What is creative living? How can we set about it?

Chapter Two

Learning to Trust

1. The first recorded prayer in the Bible was the prayer of a father for a son—Abraham for Ishmael. Make a study of other parental prayers, noting the circumstances that drew forth the prayer and the result of the prayer. What light do these records throw on the obligation of parents to pray for their children?

2. The nobleman found Jesus through the sickness of his son. Find other accounts in the Bible of benefits that came through illness. What lessons have we as individuals learned in the school of affliction?

3. "Christ's word is as good as His presence," said Bishop J. C. Ryle. What does this fact mean to us in our everyday living? In our study of the Bible?

4. Dean Inge states, "The writer of the Epistle to the Hebrews has done for Faith what St. Paul, in I Corinthians 13, has done for Love."[1] Study the eleventh chapter of Hebrews to see what it teaches of the essentials of faith. Note, too, the honor roll of "men of action." What qualities made these men worthy of being on the roll? What lessons does the author teach us through the women who are listed?

5. What is the significance of the statement: "Women received their dead raised to life again"? (Hebrews 11:35)

6. Reread Bunyan's spiritual classic: *Pilgrim's Progress.*[2] Compare the characters of Christian and Faithful.

---

[1] William R. Inge, *Personal Religion and the Life of Devotion, op. cit.,* p. 41.

[2] A "mildly modernized" version, making this immortal classic more easily understood, is available from Paraclete Press.—Ed.

7. What are some of the main difficulties of faith? What help does the Bible give us to overcome them?

8. In Hebrews 11:32-38 we have a record of faith displayed in national life. What qualities do we find in that record that should be exemplified in the leaders of a nation "conceived in liberty and dedicated to the proposition that all men are created equal"? What can we as individuals or as members of a church do to bring back righteousness as a foundation stone of our national life? What is being done about this by various groups and movements?

9. The faith of Moses as a great lawgiver forms an instructive study. List about seven qualities in Moses' character that make him a worthy hero to hold up to adventurous youth.

10. Formulate an elementary practical rule for developing the habit of praise and thanksgiving in individual lives.

Chapter Three

Restoration

1. Study carefully the ladders for youth, middle-age, and old-age in *Abundant Living* by Dr. E. Stanley Jones. If you were making a ladder for your own spiritual development, what steps would you include for your individual temperament and needs?

2. Read the "Sermon on the Mount," then try to put its instructions in a workable ladder-form that will make it mean something in your daily living.

3. What is personality? Imagine a young person coming to Jesus and complaining about the handicap of a "poor personality." In the light of your knowledge of the New Testament, can you suggest the reply that you think Jesus would make to such a person? Then contrast your Gospel list with the "Dale Carnegie" type of advice in such matters.

4. Reread chapters 1 through 20 of Jeremiah. Note the verbs used by God in commanding the prophet. Have you ever been conscious of God commanding? Now list from your own reading the commands Jesus gave to people. Are any of these commands being carried out in your daily living?

5. The Bible is full of joy. What is joy? Quote some of the outstanding occasions of "great joy" recorded in the Bible. In what did Christ's joy consist? Give specific examples from the Gospels. How can this "fruit of the spirit" be made more evident in our lives?

6. "The child is father of the man." What attitudes help us to see the sort of man that is being born of the child? Can we detect the tendencies that point to (1) the defeatist, (2) the liar or the cheat, (3) the anarchist, (4) the neurotic, (5) the able? What can be done in the way of guidance to train a child in "the way he should go"?

143

7. Read the story, "The Prodigal Son," in as many translations as possible (Luke 15:11-32). Discuss the qualities of character that led to his downfall. Note the pattern of quickening that brought about his restoration.

8. Read Romans 5:1-10. Discuss what St. Paul says here about restoration.

9. What has been your personal experience with Bible reading? Has the Bible fascinated or bored you? What impression did the Bible make upon you in your childhood? Out of your own experience have you any suggestions for making the Bible a living book to yourself and to others? What plan of Bible reading are you now following? Wherein do you find it helpful or not helpful? Be explicit.

10. Forgiveness: List about ten verses from the Bible that tell us that God will forgive our sins. What are the conditions of forgiveness? Are "conditions" compatible with the fact that forgiveness is a free gift of God? Give specific examples of individuals in the Bible who received the restoring power of forgiveness. Quote texts in which we are commanded to forgive one another. Make a list from the Bible of persons who forgave generously. Cite examples from your own experience, if possible, or from history or literature, of great "forgivers."

Chapter Four

Sustenance

1. Study the four accounts of the Lord's Supper in the New Testament: Matthew 26:26-28; Mark 14:22-24; Luke 22:19,20; I Corinthians 11:23-25. Then read John 6, which amplifies this study.

2. What does the Lord's Supper mean to you? What private preparation do you make before coming to it?

3. Collect as many definitions of prayer as you can find and see how each compares with and enriches your conception of prayer.

4. Study Chapter 3 of *Creative Prayer* by E. Herman. What suggestions given in this chapter can you use most effectively in your own practice of meditation?

5. What help have you received from great religious poetry in your practice of the Presence of God? Discuss the actual poems that have enriched your prayer life.

6. In Acts 6:4 the apostles said, "We will give ourselves continually to prayer, and to the ministry of the word." In verse 7 of the same chapter it is recorded, "And the word of God increased; and the number of the disciples multiplied in Jerusalem greatly." Discuss this statement as a revelation of the part prayer should play in evangelical work.

7. Are you a member of a prayer group? Of a prayer cell? Of a school of prayer? What about the method required for each? What can you do about conducting one or developing one in your neighborhood?

8. Jesus speaks of His gift of abundant life but also of a "straight gate" and a "narrow way" leading to it—and of the "few" who receive it. How can we reconcile contradictory terms of abundance and limitation?

9. People come to you to be fed. What would you list in order to importance as the outstanding moral needs of people today? What of their spiritual needs? How can we relate our spiritual life to the needs of others? Be specific.

10. One of our greatest educators, the late Professor Alfred Whitehead, says in *The Aims of Education:* "Moral education is impossible without the habitual vision of greatness." What do his words mean to you? Have you ever said, "Oh, I wish I could have my education all over again?" What was it that you seemed to miss on the way? What help do these Signs of the Fourth Gospel give in the creation of "the habitual vision of greatness"?

Chapter Five

Guidance

1.   Compare the three accounts of the "Walking on the Sea": Matthew 14:22-33; Mark 6:45-51; John 6:15-21 and discuss the Sign as a symbol of the unity of the Church: one vessel, one crew, one purpose, one desired haven, all working, all weary.

2.   Henry Ward Beecher said: "God comes to us in all exigencies, but never twice alike." Discuss this statement in the light of the different manifestations of Jesus as seen in these Signs.

3.   "Man's extremity is God's opportunity." Illustrate from the Gospels the help received from God in crises, and relate that help to our individual lives.

4.   What about the part played by needless fear in our lives? From examples of needless fear as shown in Matt. 17:6, Mark 4:38, Luke 1:12, what helpful instructions do we receive?

5.   Bishop Ambrose said: "We shall have to give account for our idle silences as well as for our idle words." Discuss this statement and relate it to our own lives.

6.   "Our God shall come, and shall not keep silence" (Psalm 50:3). How is this compatible with what has been said of God as a God of silence? Can you explain why Jesus answered some of the questions put to Him by His judges, and did not answer others?

7.   Read chapter three, "A New Set of Devotional Exercises" (p. 55), in *On Beginning From Within,* by Douglas V. Steere, especially the paragraphs on the spiritual exercises of St. Ignatius. In what way can your own devotional life be enriched by these exercises which he suggests?

8. The story of the Emmaus Road has been looked upon as a true pattern of procedure in meditation: Jesus takes the initiative and draws near without being recognized by the disciples; they tell Him their problem and He presents it to them in a new light; finally they recognize Him in the breaking of bread. Read the story in the Bible and then use the beautiful Emmaus Litany in *The Book of Worship* (pp. 237, 238) for guidance growing out of the meditation.

9. Newness of life is an achievement as well as a gift. It should be marked by the Christlike qualities enumerated by Evelyn Underhill: humility, detachment, poverty, love, purity, and courage. In what sense is it an achievement? Suggest definite steps in the achievement of one or more of these qualities.

10. The Greeks described a library as the "medicine chest of the soul." This phrase has been applied to the Bible. What do you know of the healing power of Jesus? Discuss the possibilities of forming a healing circle in your local church.

Chapter Six

Illumination

1. "Jesus does not throw light on scientific problems or on the problems of art or music, although these make a rich contribution to life, but He dispels the darkness that leads to despair." Discuss this statement and analyze the various aspects of the darkness that He dispels.

2. Contrast the story of the healing of Naaman (II Kings 5) with the healing of the man born blind. In what ways is the blind man's conduct a pattern for us to follow?

3. How little the Jews understood the right meaning and the worth of the Sabbath, and how little many of us understand it today! Yet the way in which we use Sunday is a sure test of our religion. How would you as a Christian explain the value and use of Sunday—what it actually means in your life—to a non-Christian?

4. Three times St. John in his Gospel tells us that the religious leaders were in "division among themselves" (7:43; 9:16; 10:19). See also Acts 5:34. Christians often stay away from meetings because they differ with the majority who attend. What can those in the minority learn from the passages just cited?

5. The Jewish mind seemed ready to accept Jesus as a "prophet." Support this with at least five illustrations from the Gospels (Matthew 21:11; 21:46; Mark 6:15; Luke 7:16; 24:19). But there was a higher step that the majority of the leaders would not take. Test our belief in Jesus in the light of these divided acceptances. "What think you of Christ?"

6. The man who had received his sight stuck to the fact that he saw: "One thing I know, that, whereas I was blind, now I see." What of the reality of the action of the Holy Spirit

149

in our lives? Can we hold fast to the fact of God's reality through His personal dealings with us?

7. In *Readings in St. John's Gospel,* the late Archbishop William Temple calls attention to the fact that there are seven parables in St. John's Gospel "of the Lord's Person introduced by the words 'I am.'" The first four "represent a comparatively external relationship, and the last three an inward vitalization." Compare the seven Signs with the seven parables (6:35; 8:12; 10:7; 10:11; 11:25; 15:1; 16:6).

8. Someone has said that this man was the first confessor who suffered for Christ's sake. What of our witness? What of our suffering for Jesus' sake?

9. Compare the occasions on which our Lord restored sight to the blind. Is there any connection between these miracles and Isaiah 29:18; 32:3; 35:5; 42:7?

Chapter Seven

Maturity

1. The return of Jesus to the place of His baptism teaches that "it is lawful to regard localities in which great spiritual works have been done with more than ordinary reverence and affection." Discuss this statement from your own experience. Have you any personal place of great memories to which you return? How does your return to it help you?

2. Compare Moses' prayer (Numbers 12:13) and Hezekiah's prayer (II Kings 19:16) with the petition of the sisters': "Lord, he whom thou lovest is sick." What can we learn from these prayers that will help us in the wise phrasing of our own?

3. This Sign teaches us what all Christians should do when they are in trouble. Contrast or compare Job 1:20 and II Chronicles 15:12 with John 11:3. What can all sisters learn from Martha and Mary?

4. Suggest practical ways in which we may "know Christ and the power of His resurrection" (Phillipians 3:10). How can knowledge help faith?

5. Discuss from this Sign and from your own experience the statement that "to show sympathy and kindness to those in sorrow is good for our own souls." Can you support the truth of this statement from other incidents recorded in the Bible?

6. Read Dr. George A. Buttrick's chapters on "The Problem of Petitionary Prayer" and "The Problem of Intercessory Prayer."[1] Discuss them in the light of the Bible teachings on prayer and from your own experience.

[1]George A. Buttrick, *Prayer* (Nashville: Abingdon-Cokesbury Press, 1942).

7. Is there a stone that is shutting your soul "into its tomb of anxiety, or worry, or resentment"? What does the lifting of that stone involve? What specific help that will encourage you to lift the stone do you get from this Sign?

8. From what dead habits can the love of God call us forth?

9. What definite help does this Sign give us as to how we may be called forth, and as to what we are to do when we have been freed from old sins or old habits?

10. Andrew Murray had some "Help to Intercession" printed in leaflet form, entitled *Pray Without Ceasing*. From his excellent pattern of intercessory prayer, or from Charles F. Whiston's book, or from some other instructions, draw up an outline of daily intercessions, covering a week. Make this practical, and test it out to see if it works. If you have not already done so, start your own book of intercessions.